GW00482918

Crannóg 57 autumn 2021

ISSN 1649-4865
ISBN 978-1-907017-63-6

Cover image: *not dealing with the important stuff*, by Milda Titford
Cover image sourced by Sandra Bunting
Cover design by Wordsonthestreet
Published by Wordsonthestreet for Crannóg magazine @CrannogM
www.wordsonthestreet.com @wordsstreet

CONTENTS

Submissions for Crannóg 58 open November 1st until November 30th
Publication date is March 31st 2023

Crannóg is published bi-annually in spring and autumn.

Submission Times:
Month of November for spring issue.
Month of May for autumn issue.

We will <u>not read</u> submissions sent outside these times.

POETRY:
Send no more than three poems. Each poem should be under 50 lines.
PROSE:
Send one story. Stories should be under 2,000 words.

We do not accept postal submissions.
When emailing your submission we require three things:
1. *The text of your submission as a Word attachment.*
2. *A brief bio in the third person, in the body of the email.*
3. *A postal address for contributor's copy in the event of publication, in the body of the email.*

For full submission details, to learn more about Crannóg magazine,
to purchase copies of the current issue or take out a subscription,
log on to our website:

www.crannogmagazine.com

We dedicate this issue to the memory of two contributors to *Crannóg*
who left us in 2022

Kathleen O'Driscoll
who died tragically in Galway
and
Simon Perchik
who died, aged 98, in Springs, East Hampton, New York

Return

tonight I saw
the four-day
moon
high over
big bare trees,
a strange
red-bottomed
black cloud
hovered briefly
then blew to the east.
I'm happy
the lemon geraniums
are flowering again ...

Kathleen O'Driscoll
excerpted from *Crannóg* 41

One Cup

One cup kept empty and side by side
as if forgiveness is a service
due when you shake the dust off

and the other overflows with coffee
heats your mouth with lips
that blacken with one hand

is grasped by the other and the spill
towed to where the dead overflow
as evenings: an entitlement

that returns the darkness
before the sun comes back ...

Simon Perchik
excerpted from *Crannóg* 54

Crannóg

Anne O'Brien

An artificial island built by the Celts, usually set in the middle of a small lake, the Crannóg contained dwellings used to house and protect a family and its livestock. A hidden underwater causeway linked the Crannóg to the mainland.

THE DRAUGHT IN THE CHIMNEY sucks the spark out before it reaches the crumpled newspapers. I strike another match and then one more. The third reaches home; the paper quickly gobbled by flames. I shut the stove door and hear the drag of wind in the chimney. When it has really taken, I pile on logs and hope the fire will hold and warm the room while I walk the shoreline.

The wind whips around the house. It's from the west and carries the low roar of the sea. For weeks now the fields have been flooded. After last night's clear sky, the pools of water are crisp at the edges. The storm has not abated, the wind is gusting gale force. Anticipation quickens in me; the tideline will be worth the battle against the blowing sand. I layer on clothes, add sheepskin gloves and a hat under my hood. The door bangs shut behind me. In minutes my face is sand-encrusted.

The laneway is impassable so I can't follow the usual path to the beach. A low lake has appeared overnight, the stunted trees shortened by their submerged trunks. I take to higher ground, ice cracking beneath my feet. The marram grass is wind-bent. I press it further into the earth, moving on before my weight causes the water to reach up and soak my boots. Pools appear wherever there is a dip, the ground water is on the rise. It has even made its way to the house, spilling up over shore grids, pooling by the front door. From day to day, I expect it to recede but instead it continues its approach, islanding me. This is no bad thing – part of me welcomes this moat.

I reach the beach, narrowed by the combination of high tide and a full moon. On the horizon, the cargo ships rise and fall and I imagine waves crashing over decks, washing down bits of rope, sauce bottles, brushes and pickle jars, all sorts of things that will, in the days to come, end up on the shoreline. It is the stranded shoes that bother me most, they are always single, well-worn and sodden. On post-storm days I find at least one on the tideline and each time I wonder how it came to be there. A shoe should be the most tethered of things.

I imagine a shipmate in oilskins, a woollen cap pulled low on his head and work gloves on his hands – I have found these too. He hauls nets, or secures cargo that has shifted in high winds, his legs apart, a balance maintained despite the roll and fall of the vessel and the gusting wind pushing from all sides – a wind that knows he is a rootless thing that can be toppled.

One gloved hand grabs the rope to steady himself while his other attempts to complete the task he's ventured out to do. The deck is wet, his work boots, old. A twisted wind and he's on his back, arm outstretched, his grip loosening on the rope. The tilted deck is the wind's ally and he is slapped against the ship's rail. The metal is all that blocks his rush to water, the force enough to suck a shoe from his foot; one minute there, gone the next.

Stunned and light-headed, he works himself to a seated position and, in the lull that follows, lashes the remaining rope on the cargo. The tarpaulin cover flaps and he knows it's unlikely it will hold. It is what it is. The cold from his sodden sock numbs his foot. He makes his way inside and heats a tin of sausages – there's bread and mustard, onions too, spare boots and dry socks. He has seen many storms.

While I walk the beach, I take the washed-up shoes and place them above the tideline. Sometimes I photograph them. They are mainly work boots, though I have also found a trainer or sailing shoe, its leather curled by saltwater. The lone shoes call to mind those lost at sea which is why I comfort myself with this story of a hardy deck-hand in spare boots, eating sausages in a galley kitchen. It helps blur other images that jostle for space in my mind's eye, images of a Greek island, a mountain of abandoned life jackets – some of which didn't do their job, rows of tents and the small industry that has sprung up converting life vests into laptop sleeves or tote bags that westerners can feel good about buying.

Things I don't want to know.

Today, there's the usual detritus on the tideline and a young seal pup too, taking a rest from the stormy waters. I spot a football boot; at least size nine, newish, lurid, fluorescent. I concentrate on not knowing, add a bit of motivated forgetting and place the shoe atop the white-painted wooden stand whose cross will hold the local authority-issue lifebelt once the summer season rolls around. The fluorescent orange is a sign now, visible from afar. But who will see it? Throughout the long winter and well into spring, this stretch of beach is deserted.

I have set a marker for myself.

I turn back, cresting the dune that separates sea from land, my pace quickening. The view is contained now, no longer stretching to the horizon and beyond, and I am glad. The dunes soon muffle the sound of waves crashing on shingle.

With the beach behind me, I look no further than home and hurry towards its shelter, across waterlogged fields, picking the path I know will hold. In haste now, like never before.

Alone in Paris Twice

Sara Backer

My solo December — living on onion soup
and the Musée D'Orsay. Constantly
cold, I drew sketches in a blank book.
Years later with a man, I felt fettered — in line
at the Louvre while he fussed with maps.
Though acrophobic, I followed his spiral
up 387 stone steps to the top of Notre Dame.
I broke down, shaking, embarrassing him.
The boat tour levelled us. Someone said *il parle*
de l'amour comme il parle de voiture. I laughed.
To be in Paris, but not in Paris — on the Seine,
drifting under bridge after bridge, lights reflected
in river dapple and in my glass of wine.
He didn't understand that I could ride this river
forever. He couldn't wait to get off.

No Stranger

Ivy Bannister

She is known in these parts as no stranger
to the tongue of sheep. I have heard her address
them myself. 'Gentle men and ladies,' she says.
The beasts freeze, but they do not startle.
Then she sings in a language I cannot fathom.
It is said that the song is rich with desire
for a dark wild man who will bring her sons
– which may or may not be – but this much I know,
her weird and beautiful notes whirl like a wind
that springs from the heart of the earth
to the crest of heaven. When it's done,
the black-snouted sheep return to their chomp
as she sails down the lane, straight-backed
in spite of her years, the mane of her hair
like a beacon brighter than the light
that burns from the sun. She passes me by
without answer to my greeting. It is said
that she thrives on blackberries and air,
and fattens her hair with sheep fluff
plucked from brambles, twisted into strands.

Last Orders

Peter Branson

For Chris Hunt

Ripe fuse of malted barley, Kentish hop,
grace notes of diesel-poisoned pollen spores,
the brewery opposite is barrelling
its golden treasury of Adam's ale.
We're open, for the breeze, to worldly things,
beyond revival-gothic leaded glass.
It overwhelms my senses, mouth and nose,
like wax and incense at Tridentine Mass.
I'm drowsy as a drunk at closing time,
pray Sister, finger to her lips, will check
her fob, a gift from parents, pleased as Punch
when she becomes a bride of Christ, and twice
as proud. She frowns, high summer afternoon,
the heavy hand-bell glinting in the sun.

Heaneyesque

Brian Harrington

at Carraig an Teampaill, An Spidéal

Far from the Flaggy Shore, on the other side of the bay,
The barnacle-freckled rocks sprawl like a beached leviathan.
Wind and light are doing their thing.
The sea interjects on occasions,
Cascading against the rocks with phlegmatic spume.
And so you resume your quiet stroll,
You do not need to stop and all that ...
Nature does its Heraclitean spin.
It's April, showers give way to spring sunlight.
Hold on tight. Water, air and light in constant flux.
You're just a dot on the horizon, you'll never get to the crux.

No Boundaries

Cassie Smith-Christmas

THE IDEA CAME TO HIM one morning as he endured her sobs through the closed bedroom door. He found himself longing for the sterile lights of his old office on Bothwell Street. Wished he hadn't taken an early retirement, or that he could turn up the TV loud enough to drown it all out.

But he didn't have the heart to do that. Instead he sat on the sofa, sipping his tea, staring at the elephants on the mantelpiece. He didn't remember exactly when she began collecting them, but once she said they were her favourite animal, they became easy gifts for Christmas, birthdays. Figurines dotted the windowsills, the dresser in their bedroom; there was even an elephant incense burner in the guest bathroom.

He set down his tea and marched to the bedroom. He pulled the door open and announced he was going to take her to see elephants in the wild. Then without waiting for an answer, he closed the door and returned to his cup of tea.

Naturally he couldn't say something like that and not go through with it. So the day afterwards he donned a suit and took the train into Glasgow Central, like the old days. He knew that most everyone else booked trips using the internet, but he was too afraid he might make a mistake.

The travel agent was a smiley wee girl but the question of where he wanted to go caught him off guard. He stared blankly and stuttered that he wanted to take his wife to see elephants in the wild. She asked him when he'd like to travel and out of habit, he answered the October holidays. She did some whirring on the keyboard and said what about Maasai Mara, in Kenya? The weather would be warm but not too hot and there would certainly be elephants. They could get a five-star package holiday, including private game drives each day. He put down his credit card, although it probably cost more than five holidays put together.

The organising became a good distraction: getting their yellow fever jabs, suitable clothes, mosquito repellent. Days now had a shape to them, a purpose. They were going to Kenya. They were going to see elephants in the wild.

———

They woke before dawn. Someone brought tea to their tent. The tea wasn't like normal tea; it had hints of liquorice, spice but he drank it anyway. When he stepped outside, the air was cooler than he expected. And dry, too, the absence of water palpable. They were ushered to the safari jeep, and the Black man who was their spotter placed red blankets on their laps.

Their guide was a White man who proudly said his family had been in Kenya since colonial times, as if somehow that fact should make two White Europeans feel safe. He started the vehicle and they were off. The safari camp was nestled in a copse beside a river, so low now it was barely a stream. They followed the indentation of the river for a while, then they were out in the open. The sun was rising, the immense sky erupting pink and yellow. The spotter stood up in the jeep, binoculars pressed to his eyes. After a while he said something to the guide and they turned towards the left, then stopped.

It was a hyena. He'd never expected to feel such affection for something he thought was meant to be so ugly. Maybe it was because it was his first animal of the safari. Or perhaps its mottled coat reminded him of Calum's Australian shepherd, the one they had all doted over. The hyena eyed them curiously, then loped away.

They stopped for breakfast in a grove of trees. He braced himself for those sorts of questions people ask when they don't know you, but thankfully, they never came. The guide was intent on frying bacon and eggs over a camp stove, the spotter busy setting up the folding chairs and little table. As they ate, the guide regaled them with stories of his boyhood in Nairobi. At one point, he told an anecdote in which the moral of the story appeared to be that one could never trust the native staff. Immediately, the spotter refilled the guide's cup of coffee.

After breakfast, they drove for a while without seeing anything. He tried to keep his eyes focused on the trees, the little spots that broke up the endlessness. It was like the sea: the grass going on until it finally collided with the blue sky. But he knew from that day in Troon that something as infinite as the sea should be avoided. They had gone to the beach because they thought it would help; it was only two months after it happened, and they were willing to try anything. But standing there, staring off into the peaks of Arran, the grey waves stretching in front of him, a hollowness took hold and he felt so overwhelmed he thought he would sob. His wife must have felt it too, for she suggested they get something to eat. They had fish and chips with lukewarm tea and a slice of bread, and then they went home, even though they didn't particularly want to. But they didn't particularly want to stay, either.

The jeep stopped. The spotter pointed to something in the distance, but it was impossible to see what he was indicating. The jeep drove on. They were going faster now, bumping over the ground towards a crest of tan-coloured hills.

The spotter said something to the guide again and they started up one of the hills, the jeep growling as they ascended. And then, they were at the top and there it was: a line of wildebeest snaking along the plain under them. The sight was magnificent and he took out the camera he had bought especially for this trip and started snapping away. The guide was grinning and slowly, he pointed to something towards the left and said, 'That's what we came up here for.'

He nearly dropped his camera. There was a lioness not more than twenty feet away, throwing her head and shuffling about, a large black mass hanging from her jaws. He realised that it was the torso of a wildebeest, the guts glittering in the sunshine, the head of the wildebeest cast to the side. The lioness paid them no mind, just continued to tear up the flesh, until at last, she lay down and dipped her face between her paws. They were close enough that he could see the fringe of blood around her muzzle.

'How did you know?' he asked the spotter.

The spotter smiled. 'I didn't. I just saw two dots, one moving towards the other. And followed them.'

After that, they started back towards the camp. The sun was high in the sky. On the way, they passed a point where the river swelled. Grey humps emerged from the brown water, and he felt bad for his wife; she craned her head excitedly out the vehicle, but they turned out just to be hippos.

———

They set out again in the late afternoon. Ten minutes into their journey there was some crackling on the two-way radio. The guide turned around and headed back in the direction of the camp, but then veered away from the river. The spotter pointed out some impala, then some kudu with their great twisted horns, and although the guide slowed down long enough for a photo, it was clear these elegant antelope were not the main attraction.

The jeep trundled along until it came upon a tree, other safari jeeps and even a small bus parked at the base. Their safari jeep nosed into the throng and the guide pointed up.

It took him a moment to realise that they were gazing at a leopard. Something else was draped across the branch where the leopard lounged. The guide said it was a duiker, that leopards sometimes liked to haul their quarries up trees.

He lifted his camera and zoomed in. He took a few snaps before noticing the red rim around the leopard's left eye. He zoomed in closer and could see clearly that there was no eye in the socket. And the duiker's tiny horns were tinged with red. He asked the guide if it was possible that the leopard had just lost its eye, and the guide replied that it was very possible. The duiker probably put up a fight.

The other vehicles eventually drove off, but theirs remained. The guide poured them their sundowner drinks. The wine was nice, but he felt a bit guilty with the leopard up there, its life now divided into Before The Incident and After, if indeed it survived with only one eye.

That night they met the other guests in the safari camp. There was the Serbian fellow with the much younger wife, and it was clear from a few remarks that the Serbian was fabulously wealthy. And then the English couple who he guessed were also retirees. It was all right at first because the dinnertime conversation stayed on the topic of the wildlife everyone had encountered that day. But then during the main course the English couple mentioned that their youngest son was twenty-seven. He knew this fact would upset his wife and he was right; after a few minutes, she excused herself to use the facilities. At night, they had to be accompanied from the dining tent by a Maasai guard with his spear, and he wondered if the guard could hear his wife sobbing through the canvas walls of the toilet building.

The pale sky was ripening to blue when they saw them. On the horizon, they looked like rocks or a clump of trees. But then it was clear what they were, their grey skin shining in the early morning light.

There were about twenty of them: different sizes, even three little baby ones springing about and waving their spindly trunks. He looked at his wife.

She was grinning ear to ear.

'They're beautiful,' she whispered. 'Absolutely gorgeous.'

She had tears in her eyes. Her smile was so bright he thought they must be tears of joy, but then her face took on that faraway look. She pulled her sunglasses over her eyes and turned her head away from the elephants.

It must be the babies, he thought. Any reminder of that sacred bond. Calum had been twenty-six when they received the phone call about the crash on the M8. He'd been driving home for Sunday lunch and for weeks, the only words she could utter were why didn't he take the train, or, if only she hadn't asked him to pick up a thing of Bisto from the big Tesco on his way.

He felt a swell of anger: did it know no boundaries, this grief? Couldn't it just allow his wife a few moments' respite, here in the middle of the Maasai Mara, a thousand miles from home, seeing her favourite animals in the wild?

He could get a few photos at least. Avoid the babies, of course; but the more he tried to get a few without them, the more they were everywhere. He snapped one of a baby with its trunk stretching up into the curve of its mother's mighty shoulder. The light was soft, giving a sort of halo effect to their two rounded bodies. It was probably one of the best photos he'd ever taken.

His wife turned her head. He could see the trails of tears from the corners of her sunglasses. Yet a smile bloomed on her face again. 'They're truly gorgeous, aren't they?'

He nodded. The jeep rumbled on. He stared out at the landscape but instead of focusing on the spots, he let himself be consumed by the endlessness of it all.

Michelangelo

David Starkey

You, Caravaggio,
              baptized Michelangelo
Merisi, born on the feast day
of the archangel, wawling
in candlelit darkness, as the blood
dries on your cradle cap.
                    Late September
1571, Christendom
battling Suleiman the Magnificent,
the world, as always, in turmoil,
though your petite bourgeoise family
is more concerned with scudi
and distinction than the fate of man.

How unlikely that you, or anyone,
would wend his way from infancy
through the byzantine corridors
of childhood and manhood to shoulder up
against that other Michelangelo, equally
staggered by his singularity.
                    Still,
that's years away. Let this particular day
have its moment – the nurse fumbling
with the coverlet in your crib,
your mother exhausted and dozing
in another room, your father brooding
by a fire kindled on the cusp of autumn.

Domesticity

Noelle Sullivan

This house could be a ravine
winding in on itself. The fallen sock on floor
maps a story of someone undressing in the dark
so as not to disturb others. At foot, small boulders
of toys left in their wake, a rush of water
from a storm or tiny breezes near
an oxygen machine making possible
a sky of dreams.

I let the clothes drown in the gravel wash,
feel leaves brush elbows, the scent of clay
running over me in sheets, dust pouring into lines
of careworn carving. I'll rest, Pompeiian,
until our lips finally meet as two unmoving stones,
outward walls against the searing heat,
dyke of determination.

We'll make a shelter from scorched ash
and falling water — we two, hoodoos,
no pillars of society. Come, live as the land
with me. Live as stone.

Wren and the Death of Shona

Martin Towers

Wren?
Yes?

You're quite a thing aren't you?
I am, yes. Were you watching me?

I watched you go over to the far bank. To the wall.
I watched you flick around in last year's growth.

Yes. I maintain separateness through smallness, fleetness.
I do not attend birdfeeders.

Did you take the shells
left out as offerings as the dark night came on?

I did. For missing Shona.
Did you plait them into her hair as she floated in the river?

Yes. As dawn came.

Dear Friend

Daragh Byrne

i.m. Janet McKechnie

What good does a letter do? Faintly printed Courier New
informs you that your insurance claim has been rejected; that
the paternity test was inconclusive; that a motorway is to be
built through your front room. And yet — there is the perfume
of the pillowed love-note; the cash in a card from a distant aunt;
the scout camp scribbles to your mother admitting that you miss
her cooking. When you share in the group chat that the only
thing they can do is buy me more time, I imagine your words
dying with the devices they were born on. I dig out a pen from a
drawer. My handwriting sprouts from the page like copper
wires from the guts of a broken dynamo. I ask if you still think
of those August dawns breaking over Edinburgh — the
tangerine tip of each new day feathering the grey fade of the
night before; the gin spilled in your handbag. I am careful with
my tense. I do not mention your prognosis; how your future
reroutes itself, how it brandishes a handless clockface at you
and says tick. You are radiant in my remembrance. Perhaps I
can remind you to read between the lines while you still can. I
am writing with so little time left. I am writing to keep you
alive.

The Snow Globe

Justine Carbery

SHE CHECKS ONCE MORE that no-one is looking, puts the key in the lock and turns. A soft click and she's in. *In the belly of the whale* she thinks, while her breathing returns to normal and the clutter of her bones reassembles itself into something less dangly than a pocketful of keys. The silence is thick and gluey and she moves nothing but her eyes, lest she disturb the molecules of air thrumming across her downy skin. *He lives here now* she thinks. *Here.* Not at home with his kids, with me, not in our big house by the sea with the bright red door and brass knocker, where the hallway streams with early-morning light, refracting in ribbons of blue and yellow and ruby red. *Our very own cathedral* he'd said their first morning in that house, when they rose, crumpled with sleep, padding down the stairs, too raw and love-bruised to speak in full sentences yet. Pooled in the diffusion of stained glass light. *Our Notre Dame,* he'd said, *our Chartres.* And he'd kissed her there amidst the floating dust-mites, the warm light varnishing them, the hot iron of desire flaring through them once more.

The memory bows her, then belches her into this hallway, *his* hallway. What the fuck was she doing here? What the hell had she been thinking? Stevie had pressed the key into her hand, whispering,

-Go, Mum. I want you to know where we disappear to on Wednesday nights.

She'd had to swallow the slick of bile rising in her throat.

-Go on, take a quick look, see what we see. Then leave. Simple.

Simple? As simple as untangling the Christmas lights, or combing the knots out of Katie's hair. As simple as leaving your wife of twenty years.

And yet here she is, gulping mouthfuls of stale air in a hallway that's colourless and cold, heart pounding like the frantic churr of a frightened nightjar. She takes three tentative steps along the hall. A door is half-open, the maw of it luring her in. The bedroom is small and grey, an unmade double bed, Ian McEwan's *Atonement* tented on a white bedside locker. She blushes, unzipped by the ordinariness of it all; the lumpy duvet heaped and mounded like sand-dunes, the pillow creased and shaped in a C. She tries not to look, not to notice the stripy boxers crumpled on the floor. She can picture him stepping out of them, the half-moons of his buttocks disappearing into the bathroom, the hiss and hiccup of the shower as it spurts into life.

She shouldn't be here, she knows that, but she cannot move, her body welded to the doorjamb, her breath coming in rapid, shallow gasps. He sleeps here. With her, that honey-pot woman, who'd enticed him away. Sleeping with her, beside her, in her, sharing fluids, stories, dreams. Not back in their bay-windowed bedroom, with the fairy-lights and duck-egg drapes, the flimsy light filtering through. Not spooning her curved body, the space between them as thin as skin.

Pain seeps through her like water through sand, and she feels both saturated and scraped out, memories leeching the marrow from her bones. The air in the room is dry as dust, and she steps over the fallen boxers to the bathroom. A thin layer of scum fronds the white porcelain. The taps and mirror are spattered with flecks of toothpaste. Two toothbrushes. She dry-retches into the sink.

Her phone pings in her pocket, jolting her out of a stupor. Christ. She can't deal with anyone. Not here. Not now. She tries to ignore the insistent ring and the vibrating against her leg. She stumbles out of the bedroom, looks around, faintly disappointed and faintly pleased that there isn't much else to see. A nondescript office to the left. A large living/dining room to the right. Insubstantial voices filter through the walls, the jingle of a radio show, the muffled cry of a baby. Once again, the thought comes to her; what on earth is she doing here?

Take a quick look, see what we see. Then leave.

What does she hope to find amidst the clutter on the dining room table, the toast-crumbed breakfast plates on the kitchen bar, the coffee-ringed cups. Two of everything. His and hers. What did she expect? She suppresses the image of them breakfasting together, kissing goodbye at the door.

He'd given up kissing her a long time ago. In a way, she was just as glad. The thought of his tongue, all wet and loose, cartwheeling in her mouth makes her want to gag again. And yet, it pains her in her heart and bones to think of *them*, slick with sweat, bucking and arching, until spent with lust, they lie cradling each other. How dare he? How dare he let her go, cast her adrift, like a creaky boat unfit for purpose, traded-in for a younger model?

Granted, the sex hadn't been great. More like a chore really, like emptying the dishwasher or ironing the sheets. Since when? she wondered. When did it become such a clockwork, mechanical thing? No eyes. No tongues. Just grinding and shuddering and rolling over. With the advent of kids? Since his promotion and long hours at the office? Since caring for elderly parents and demanding teenagers had worn her thin, like a dishcloth ready for the bin? But there had been other times when the sex had worked. That family holiday in Greece. Mid-afternoon and all the kids were making pirate costumes for a game of Castaway. She went back to their room to get suncream, leaving the soft curve of the beach, and entering the shadowed dark of the wooden chalet. He'd followed her, shutting out the daylight as he leaned against the door. In the damp darkness she could smell his want, steaming off him, like vinegary chips. She'd bent to open the travel bag and suddenly he was behind her, the girth of him pressing into her thin bikini. His hands, roughened and welted from sailing, sought out her curves, tore at the strings, loosening everything, including her. It was over quickly, just the warm pant and heft of him, the prick of desire cresting in her.

'Here, take this down to the beach, will you,' she'd said, handing him the cream, as he re-toggled his swimming shorts around his waist. 'I'm taking a shower.' And he left, without speaking, particles of sand peppering the floor where they'd stood.

Her phone rings again, skittering her heart.

-Mum, where are you? I can't find my maths book.

-Katie, she wrestles the words from her mouth like toffee. -Sorry, love. I don't know. Didn't you put it back in your bag after your homework?

-I didn't have any maths homework. We had a free period. I did it then.

-Well, maybe you left the book in your locker. As she spoke, Sarah's eyes scanned Dermot's bookshelves. Mostly what he'd taken with him, leaving gaping holes in her collection. Thick histories of Stalingrad, Vichy France, the 1916 Rebellion. How to Get Rich Quick. A few new ones. A Booker nominee. A Guide to Wicklow Hillwalking. A diabetes cookbook.

-Mum, are you listening?

Diabetes

-Mum, what's going on? Where are you?

Sarah pressed her hand to her forehead. Dermot didn't have diabetes. Or did he? Had this happened recently and she didn't know?

-Out, Katie.

-Well, obvs.

Or was it for *her*? Sarah didn't like to think of *her* being real. She didn't like thinking of her at all.

-Mum, you're being weird. Gotta go or I'll be late. Before Sarah could answer, Katie was gone. Beads of sweat braceletted her forehead, her armpits, the small of her back. She had to get out. This was crazy. What on earth had Stevie been thinking? *Take a quick look, see what we see.* At the thought of her 17-year-old son, she smiled. Such a kind boy, a young man really. About to finish school and head out into the big bad world. So thoughtful. So sensitive. He'd taken the split very hard at first. That terrible day they sat the kids down to tell them Dad was moving out. He needed time. It was complicated. Stevie's eyes like saucers. Katie already weeping silently.

-I've met someone, Dermot said in a half whisper. Through her rage Sarah could still make out his discomfort, his distress at hurting them.

-What do you mean you've met someone? Stevie said, rising to his feet, towering over Dermot, hunched on the edge of the window seat. He looked up at Stevie, his eyes pleading with him.

-Are you fucking her? Is that what you mean? There was no mistaking his anger now, betrayal and hurt crushing his skinny frame. His voice was hard, his Adam's apple jumping conspicuously in his throat. Outside the wind and rain vied with each other, hurling themselves against the window as if to force entry.

'Stevie!' Dermot's voice cracked. Stevie shook his head, as if trying to dislodge water from his ear.

'Whatever.' He didn't wait to hear any more, storming from the room, like a Fury, slamming the door as he left. The walls rattled, and Sarah's bones. Katie had made herself quiet and small, as if trying to disappear through the slits in the floorboards. Tears like fat raindrops fell on the brown leather couch, and they all watched silently as they ran in tiny rivulets to the creases where the broken crisps and lost hair clips reside.

Suddenly Sarah wants to punch something, a wall, a cupboard, a door. Or take the flimsy curtains and tear them to shreds. Or the stupid yellow cushions on the stupid purple couch. How could he? How could he do that to his own children? How could he do it to her?

On the fireplace over the fake fire, she spots something. A small snow globe. In it a white owl with beady eyes and fierce bushy brows v-eed across the forehead. She'd bought it for Dermot after a falconry session they'd done to celebrate their twentieth wedding anniversary.

The first bird on display had been a goshawk, a huge feathered thing, as muscled as a boxer, gnarly talons clenched, fiery eyes scanning the horizon like heat-detecting missiles. Sarah's arm strained under the grey-feathered weight of it, and when it flew, its broad barred wings seemed to fill the sky.

Next up was the great grey owl, its flat silvery face like a satellite dish, its large surprised eyes surveying the pasture. In the handler's scuffed leather satchel were tidbits; mice, day-old chicks, a vole. Pink and raw. He proffered a pale skinless mouse, but Dermot's phone rang, and distracted, he let the foetus-like scrap fall from his hand. With a sudden silent whoosh that Sarah felt along the outer membrane of her skin, the owl swooped low, landing noiselessly on the carcass, tearing flesh from bones with a ferocity that startled her. Dermot fumbled with his phone, apologising, a scarf of red rising up his face.

She'd bought the snow globe in the gift shop on the way out and given it to Dermot that evening, along with a card that read Happy Anniversary My Darling Husband.

The card was long gone, she suspected, but the owl remained, eyeing her suspiciously, from its perch. She had a momentary impulse to smash it to bits. She could just see it, the liquid pooling on the granite hearth, the owly figurine disintegrating, the glass splintering into smithereens, Dermot's stricken face. But no, she picks it up and slowly shakes, churning the glittery particles, scattering soundlessly in space. She watches, dewey-eyed, as the snow swirls to the bottom, the flittering fragments clearing and settling on the frozen ground, the air silent and soft.

A Happy Man

Rachel Coventry

The men of my childhood were unhappy.
They wore suits and smoked cigarettes.

They never cried but one died
frozen on a park bench.

One, I visited in a psychiatric hospital
made pictures with nails and thread.

Although my grandfather seemed content
his lungs were black in his chest.

The men of my youth played chess
in a bedroom room, listening to punk.

They planned how to hang themselves,
scratched ciphers into their flesh.

Later on the men I knew were drunk
or numbed-out in some other way.

One told me he didn't understand love –
but by then it was way too late.

Wood Gatherers

Timothy Dodd

Out of the ground also comes
limb, as beech, pine would, but
for the silver-eyed in silhouette.
Risen from the blackest soil,
coal-fed, cramped, pallor pole,
they hover, wave, and flicker
steadfastly, as if tree-rooted,
their glow defying expectation
and logic, a blur between stasis
and stirring, figures drifting
in some space neither free nor
captured. As with a pale haunt
from the white birch's reaching
arms, you will not stay a night
on this hillside hanging. But
for them, something says to stay.
Something tells them leaving
is a loss of everything. Carrying
on in shadow sway, the longing
are forces floating from our dead,
reflections of the dappled light.

Some People

Barbara Dunne

After Rita Ann Higgins

Some people prefer the ways things used to be,
how the world turned not around the sun but
revolved around a self-centred universe.
How trams used to run over cobbled streets,
how we only ever ate strawberries in June,
and tins of Roses only ever appeared at Christmas.

Still others hanker after former glories, like when
Jackie's Army stormed the stadium in Stuttgart,
to settle old scores. I hung over my father's shoulder,
watching the battle unfold. Then, there are some,
who lust for blood, and the thrill of terror,
as one longs for ice-cream on a sunny day.

Forecast

Geraint Ellis

I used to breathe –
I think –
before you came and changed the weather.
Lying in the sea foam
of your cloudy cotton sheets
I'd watch
you dangle your arm in amber air
to let the dawn light grip
your thumb and finger
like a newborn.
Through giggling fits you'd call it your sun hand
and, washed in the sea spray from your small lisp and lilt,
I'd forget I hadn't sipped the air for hours.
Perhaps we're underwater,
with a seething ocean overhead
hushed by the laugh from your lips
and suddenly stalled,
as you break the surface with an outstretched limb,
pointing skywards,
to give the stars directions
to teach the cosmos how to spin.

Between Sleeping and Waking

Attracta Fahy

We also live in our dreams; we do not live only by day.
Sometimes we accomplish our greatest deeds in dreams.
~Carl Jung, *The Red Book*, 242.

Her visits were always in the in-between space.
A presence between asleep and awake,
always between sleeping and waking,
a voice to the right foot of my bed,
a self-assured voice at the foot of my bed.
The dream told me to 'go to the forest'
Her voice in my dream said, 'go to the forest',
her words a vibration from crown to root,
words vibrating through crown to root,
afraid at first that she was an enemy.
Took years to trust she wasn't the enemy
led me into the forest in quest of myself,
a quiet presence, the innocent self.
Her visits were always in the in-between space.

Begin

Dolores Walshe

SO KICK YOURSELF FOR SEARCHING ONLINE again, finding pictures of Alan in ecstasy with the twenty-something he betrayed you for last year a whole year Rosie and you're still jealous besotted bewildered unable to live in your own skin so get out of the house cross the yard ignore the ailing cherry blossom you planted this spring, seize the moment, a cycling trip with the Gapp twins is better than an all-day all-too-familiar traipse through the labyrinth of Ma's past, her youth eternally present to her now while the rest of her hippocampus dwells in soap operas, period dramas, so hup on the saddle girl, pedal through your desperation out the shortest route on the back road, crossing re-crossing the border, oh the luxury of peacetime, nail yourself to these ditches bloated with cow-parsley, meadowsweet, inhale more fragrance than the Chanel Alan bought you no, oust him from your head, but doesn't Sergeant Hannigan do it for you, swerving out of his lane on his Raleigh Striker, yelling how great a morning it is for the cycle while you crush teeth, choking on your disappointment, what dumb way did you check the station roster last night, certain he'd be on duty today, eff it anyway, forced now to smile it out, but Hannigan casts you a suspicious look, eyes dense as turf, the rest of him blue, like he doesn't get enough of it in the force, jeans, socks bicycle-clipped, blue shirt steamrolled flat, creases sharp as a jealous tongue though there's nobody to be jealous of since his wife Gráinne died three years back when, the twins say, Hannigan lost his mass of blue-black hair, explaining now how he swapped shifts with young Henry, couldn't resist the chance of a cycle when he heard the twins were planning a trip to Carrick, you silent, letting the swallows flitting ahead from ditch to ditch take over the conversation till you arrive at the pub, throwing your bike against the low wall separating forecourt from road, the twins already there, biker-shorted T-shirted, sprawled on benches enjoying a beer, legs forested in hair tinged with the frost of middle-age, something you're not far off yourself, Tom Gapp announcing young Paudie's been here looking for you Rosie, while of course Boy Blue sets his bike methodically into the rack alongside the twins' saying he caught *that little effer* walking out of Flood's yesterday carrying a Magnum, you swivelling, bug-eyed, asking if it was loaded before you can stop yourself, Jesus, you say, he's only fourteen, and the twins guffaw, oh yeah, loaded alright, with chocolate, y'know the chunky layered kind with raspberry ice-cream he's fond of spiriting from the petrol shop, *that* kind of weapon, and even Hannigan laughs while you pretend to root in your basket, raspberry now yourself, this'll do the rounds of the station, the stations in the next few towns and even some north of the border, no you'll never again have street cred but it's then Terry says well speak of the devil and in the crevice between him and Tom you catch sight of Paudie kicking a stone down the road towards you, spotting the men, stopping dead, shoulders clenching as he eyes Hannigan, but leaning out you wave at him and he waves madly back, kicking the stone again, coming towards you as Hannigan looks up, noticing him, that little effer he snarls again, and before you know it you're snarling back that *he'd* be a bloody big effer himself if he was living in Paudie's hell-pit part of town so could he try saying young-fella instead, though on second thoughts it might scald his tongue, at which the twins gaze upwards as if there's a sudden cloud formation of vital interest, while a dark stain spreads across Hannigan's cheeks as he stares at you in the lengthening pause, Terry starting to whistle as you brace yourself, he'll put you down for every night duty available after this, every dull task, that's if he doesn't have you disciplined, but instead he turns to the twins, tone overly polite, asking would anybody like a lemonade and without waiting for an answer he strides across the forecourt into the pub while Terry asks if you want to spoil the morning's cycle, you pointing out all Hannigan's good for is passing judgement in his impeccable shirts and doesn't this set Tom off, leaning towards you eager to do your head in with the usual shite of how Boy Blue only irons his shirts to feel close to his dead Gráinne on account of her liking him always smelling of her freshly ironed clothes, but they add in a little dig this time, sure haven't you been there yourself Rosie, losing a husband if you don't mind us saying, and they sit back finally, sending their clodhopper sympathy your direction, you burying the sting in your basket again, pretending to search for your water bottle, do they suspect you lied to them when you transferred back home to live with Ma, telling them you'd fallen out of love with Alan when in reality he and the young-one were already chewing the flesh off each other in their new quayside apartment in Galway, had the Gapps too been trawling the internet, the obvious answer to this crushing you, so turn now towards Paudie arriving, how's your mother, Paudie, force a smile to entice him into the forecourt, stick-skinny, teeth needing repair, hair a thatched roof, all earnest-eyed, asking did your puncture stay fixed Rosie, did I fix it right and you smile despite yourself at his long loving looks at your bike, sure get up on it, Paudie, test it for yourself, and in an instant he's astride it grinning his head off, riding around the forecourt, rearing the front wheel skywards, hands in his pockets, the twins hooting at him, all of you laughing till he passes the pub door as Hannigan comes out, swerving to avoid him, spilling his lemonade, calling him a little cur, ordering him off *your* bike, threatening to level him but Paudie laughs, taking his cue from what's in your face, telling Hannigan he wouldn't be able to catch him even if he was fit enough and you run forward as Hannigan slaps his glass down on a table and strides towards Paudie but Paudie's back up on the saddle in an instant, pedalling past you out the gate, Paudie, you yell, and it's swallowed in the twins' laughter as they tell Hannigan there's a gauntlet for him now, but Hannigan's already up on his own bike, haring out of the yard on a string of curses as you screech that you gave Paudie permission, but he's gone, so you grab one of the bikes out of the rack, swing your leg over the bar, if he gets his hands on Paudie he'll kill him and you hear Tom roaring he'll go instead of you but already you're out on the narrow road, pedalling hard, rounding the bend to be belted in the face by an overhanging branch of hawthorn in blossom, the pair of them ahead now on the straight stretch, moving fast, Hannigan gaining on Paudie but suddenly Paudie starts to wobble as if he's struck something, veering off into the ditch, somersaulting over the handlebars, disappearing, a clatter of birds rising in protest and by the time you arrive Hannigan's crashing through the brambles at the bottom of the ditch, making towards Paudie lying face down below, Jesus Paudie, you screech, heart rattling till slowly he lifts his head, shakes it, and you breathe again, Hannigan heaving too, all weird grunts as he reaches Paudie, hauls him up, tosses him your way out of the ditch, you biting out how this is all his fault as you pull Paudie out onto the road, muck-streaked, ripped T-shirt, scratches on his face, is he alright, hurting anywhere, but he's looking at you penitent, shame-faced, already picking up your bike with its buckled wheel, promising he'll pay for it, chop wood wash dishes, whatever y'want, okay Rosie, though you're just glad he's alive, his head's in one piece, and before you can speak there's a groan behind and when you turn it's Hannigan, shrivelled diminished collapsed sitting in a sunburst of wild iris like he's someone's idea of the booby prize at a farmer's mart, chest juddering like an ailing Simmental under streaks of mud, staring at his feet, blood trickling down his cheek, is he having a heart attack or what, Gráinne, he whispers hoarsely all glazed-eyed and the anger drains out of you listening to his breath hissing, steam from a geyser as he gets more sounds out, how he thought he'd killed him, raising his head now, agonised, looking right through you into an abyss as Paudie, stepping back terrified, stutters that he didn't kill him at all but you mouth to the boy to keep quiet, to take the bike home for you, you'll sort things out tomorrow, Paudie nodding, hurrying off as you sit beside Hannigan in the ditch till eventually he calms enough, words, then, streaming out of him, low and even, how a couple of years back, before the peace, cycling home in near-dawn light after his first night duty he came upon them executing a boy, gagged, kneeling, blindfolded, before the headlights of their truck, hands tied behind his back, how casually they slung him into the ditch, Hannigan hiding till they drove off, then climbing down to the boy, and the way he bares his teeth on a whine tells you the rest as he tries to lever himself up, so you rise, offering him your hand, ashamed at how you've had it in for him, his stout fingers trembling in yours, on his feet at last, whey-faced, unsteady, you can't let him go like this, you're not far from your place, there's brandy in the house so wheel his bike, avoiding the broken spokes as he sighs, falling meekly into step, you warning him your ma's developed dementia, him nodding, yes he's heard, sure his own da thought he was the czar of Russia, both of you relieved the conversation's turned towards madness, your bike there where Paudie's left it in the yard against the cherry blossom while indoors, Irene the carer is delighted getting off early and Ma's delighted with Brendan Hannigan, calling him Mister Darcy as she puts the kettle on, you sloshing brandy into his cup, muttering how she's stuck this week on this actor on TV, but he's up to speed on *Pride and Prejudice,* hasn't he five sisters living around him like a herd of satellites, that fella's all they can talk about and he downs the brandy as if to fortify himself against another Darcy onslaught, downs the next one too, weathering tea, scones and Ma's imagination with a courtesy that startles, and later, stepping into the scald of sunshine in the yard, after an awkward pussyfooting moment he uses

Paudie's name, telling you he's fast on the bike, that he could fix up his da's for him, it's not exactly the czar's horse but it'd do him rightly he says, eyes narrowing on his next idea, sure he might even *train* Paudie, if he's interested, and he raises an eyebrow as if seeking consent, oh you'll run it by Paudie for sure you say, thanking him, but he tells you he's the one's grateful, voice dredging gravel, wearing his wife's faithfulness pressed about him, the broken spokes of his bike ticking against the wheels as he weaves off down the lane and you turn away fast, gutted yet glad at the purity of his grief as you're brought up short by the little tree, finally noticing its leaves nodding above you parched as your heart and it's then it dawns on you you've never watered it, that this's maybe where you could begin

At the Konzert Haus

Bernie Crawford

The English translation said 'divest yourself
of outer garments'. *Just our coats?*
I mimed another layer but was frowned upon.

In the awesome grandeur
of the *Ludwig Van Beethoven* room
I mingled with others accordingly divested.

They were mostly dressed in black, forty shades of.
I wore a flare of orange around my neck, sipped
the proffered glass, but I was out of place:

the free concert was three floors up, under
the sloping roof, in the *Kleine Salle*. Everyone here
was still robed in outdoor clothes.

Because they hadn't been similarly divested
I couldn't see the clout of their undergarment.
Some, I suspect, were colourful.

Bearing Down

Jessamyn Fairfield

Before we reach the hospital,
it starts as a familiar pain,
smouldering like a coal seam
no longer dormant
in the cracked ground.
The distant, volcanic roar
comes closer as the hidden
path ignites.

Echoes of animal cries
in the searing air —
I am burning,
popping with heat;
spruce trunks blister apart,
catching faster in each gasp,
and matter turns to ash,
heat, and light.

Flames are crowning
across canopied trees,
each brief blaze of thorny resin
obliterates path, shapes, self;
flash after flash, unbearably bright,

bursting open, blind —
the slap of damp earth
in a rush of blood
awakens
the wailing life in my arms.

Sunday Afternoon

Mary Ellen Hodgins

Power washers buzzing all morning
pavements blitzed white, my dogs
sniff with suspicion

Sunday everywhere, the quietness of
empty streets, front doors shut firmly
a familiar loneliness

A neighbour admires his tumble of
roses from street side, he does not like
animals, the dogs know this

At the corner, the musty meadow smell
of weed hangs in the lifeless air, boys
in sun shades, half in, half out of the
world

The hours stretch out, there is nothing
else, but the crowded memory of other
Sundays, other towns, other lives.

In a Portrait of James Joyce

Mary Melvin Geoghegan

Jacques-Emile Blanche (1934)

Something is lurking
Joyce seated in a three-quarter view
turning slightly towards us.
The angle is deliberate.
He could be concerned
a frontal pose might accentuate:
the thick lenses of his glasses
proof of a failing eyesight.
And in his face a captured tension
that renders the sitter weary.

Joyce never liked the portrait
perhaps, revealing too much
as he later remarked
'awful, except for the splendid
tie I had on'.

No Map Back

Jean O'Brien

There is no map back to childhood
or to our children's childhood. We have to
rely on the unreliable, that slippery thing,
memory. No cartographer ever sat and drew
the lines, nor followed the contours of the years
or delineated the seas and the borders
of our world or reminded us *Here Be Monsters*
and indeed there were and are.

No one thought back then to coordinate
the stars, the celestial sky, we could have
perhaps pinpointed an exact time and place.
Sometimes we catch a glimpse through the gauzy veil,
a sudden flash of illumination, the palimpsest of years.
A much loved red trike, Mother putting on lipstick,
protruding her lips in a *moue*, a kiss —
one of my children twirling arms outstretched,
the world a blur, a long silence echoing still.

Song for Swallows

Eileen Casey

ON THE WAY BACK FROM SITTING by the water, staring across at Manhattan's skyline or watching people throw tennis balls for their dogs, I stop off at the Hippy Store. A bell tinkles as I prise the door open. A musical sound, pleasant to the ear. But it's that kind of sensual setting. Soft lights, silky smells, ornamental wind-chimes suspended from the ceiling. That same song playing, the same one as the last time I was here. The time before that too.

'Ink Spots. They're the guys who sing it. It's an early recording. 40s.' The voice belongs to the owner of the store ... at least I'm guessing he's the owner. Usually hovering behind the counter, today he's stocking shelves. Tarot cards. Fairies. Oils. He's noticed me pause in my browsing to listen to the words of the song.

'I didn't know,' I reply, which is the truth. 'The melody is sort of ...' I search for just the right word but he beats me to it.

'Melancholy?'

'Yes, that's it,' I say, 'that's it exactly.'

'I play it a lot, it's kind of soothing.' He looks into my eyes but not in an appraising way. His glance is one of curiosity which I find oddly pleasing. It makes me less conscious of the damp patches under my arms. I dab at my face with a tissue.

'July in New York ... they're not kidding,' he says and shows me a bright smile. His teeth are white and even.

'It's pretty cool in here though,' I say. 'Cool air and cool objects. Hard to imagine though ... especially where I come from ... shutting the door to keep the cool air in and the heat out.' I realise I'm blabbering so I stop talking.

He glides towards the counter as if on wheels. I've seldom seen such an elegant mover, especially for a heavyset man. Probably a great dancer too. He blends into the shop in a chameleon kind of way, his aquamarine kimono is the exact same shade as the walls. I'll buy some candles. It would be awkward to leave empty-handed, especially as I've struck up a conversation of sorts. Besides, I *do* need a gift for Ruby. After all, I've been sleeping in her bed for the past week. I'll get some for Ellie too, she's always liked pretty candles and, as her cat mostly sleeps on the end of her bed, her room could probably do with a shot of Jasmine.

I hand him the two packs of four rainbow-coloured, scented candles and he begins to wrap each pack in crinkly tissue.

'Know where Capistrano is?' he asks, 'I'm thinking you're Irish?'

'Yes, I'm here visiting my daughter. And no, I haven't an idea.' That's as much information as I'm willing to give about Ellie. She's asked me never to discuss anything about her with others. Especially strangers.

'It's in California. Swallows have been flying there for as long as anyone can recall,' he says. His hands splay out on the counter top. Elegant hands with slender fingers. 'Same as anyplace, I guess. They leave and then, just when you're about to forget all about them, they come back.' He shrugs his broad shoulders and then gives me the packages. I pay with crisp dollar bills.

'Those Capistrano birds are cliff swallows,' he continues, 'nesting in the scree, then bam! Out over the clear blue they go.' His right arm shoots out in a sweeping motion. 'Takes guts to make that leap,' he says on a wistful note. I nod and turn away. His eyes have a far-away look in them, already I've faded into another sale. The bell tinkles again as I leave the shop, notes of the song following me out onto the pavement.

When you whisper farewell in Capistrano, that's the day you'll come back to me. My head fills up with images of blue-winged birds darting into spring cliff-tops and darting out over the sea again in autumn.

I walk by regimental rows of windows facing out onto the street. Air-condition units slot into wooden frames as if they're window boxes, not machines. Growing cool air, not scarlet geraniums or begonias. Almost mid-morning and so hot that it seems as if the buildings have skin. Paint peels and blisters. I stop off at the deli to buy a carton of milk and soda. I'm tempted to get a cone but have learnt the hard way that ferocious heat sluices ice-cream through fingers. Not a good look, as Ellie says.

Soon I'm back outside Ellie's apartment block. The front door is like a Rosetta stone for graffiti artists. Every inch covered in either symbols or letters. Nothing makes much sense. Frankie is in his usual spot, the window seat way three floors up. It's hard to imagine that cat's never felt grass or climbed a high tree. Or that Ellie finds nothing odd or sad about it. Still. That cat is all she'd left of a bad break-up but at least she's out of that situation. 'Amen,' I say aloud, grateful for small mercies.

By the time I reach the third flight of stairs, the muscles in my thighs are screaming. Droplets of sweat roll down my back. The apartment pretty much seems to be perched on top of a cliff itself. My chest tightens and I clutch the banisters for support. These stairs are a daily ordeal, especially after the subway, rushing through turnstiles, down to the platform, then up more stairs to daylight. Of course Ellie thinks I'm forever young. But these stairs! Especially the stairwell on the second level. That mutt growling on cue each time anyone passes by his master's door. In my mind I imagine him as the three-headed monster guarding Hades. We never see any of the other tenants, just sounds at odd hours. Only a week ago Ellie lugged my heavy suitcase up and down two subways from the airport. And these three flights. Despite her thinness and small frame, she still has the Amazonian strength she's always had. I wait a few minutes outside her apartment door so when I go in I'm not breathless and gasping like a fish out of water.

Once inside, I'm guessing Ellie must be sleeping still, her bedroom door, which opens onto the living room, is closed. I hadn't heard her come in from her bar shift, testimony to how exhausted I must have been. In a low tone I sing the line, *When the swallows come back to Capistrano ...*

'Where the fuck is Capistrano?' Ellie says with her familiar directness as she comes out of the small kitchenette. It's a 'trait' I'm guessing she's picked up in the bar where she works. With her hair tousled and her pale face free of make-up, she looks drained, every inch the thirty-year-old woman she is. Five years since moving to New York and still 'figuring out' how to get the elusive green card so she can come home. Only a few more days left before everything goes back to normal. Ruby returned from her vacation in Florida and into her bed in Brooklyn and me on a plane to Dublin.

'It's in California,' I say. I bought some candles in the Hippy store near the water and the song was play —'

'Did you remember the milk?' she interrupts. Ellie's lack of enthusiasm stops me in mid-sentence so I bite back a retort about rudeness and put the carton on the table. Frankie swirls around her bare legs and she picks him up, cooing to his purr as if he were a baby.

For the hundredth time at least I wonder what it is about being here that so beguiles her. Long nights working late shifts, daylight slept away in a cramped apartment. No matter how I try to square it, I can't solve the riddle. Maybe it's just the guilt I'm feeling that makes me so uneasy? Ellie's taken some time off work so we can sight-see together. But she still has to earn her rent and utilities. I'm not sure how many more times either I can scale those stairs. Not to mention the stepdown at the bathroom door which, if I forget is there, will mean a nasty fall and God knows what cost of trouble. And definitely, I'm never coming again in high summer.

'How was last night?' I ask, in a light tone that belies the turmoil in my head. I start setting out the bowls and cutlery I'd left on the table earlier.

'The first few hours were pretty dead but it livened up after that. Some of my big tippers came in so all's good.' She begins to spoon sugar on her cereal. I know by her expression that question time is over regarding work, that she still resents me saying, one time, *one time*, that she didn't need her first-class degree for bar work.

'How're the dog people by the water?' she asks, between mouthfuls.

'Still throwing tennis balls. Some have babies so they throw and rock the pram, all at the same time. Gosh, those dogs sure love the taste of tennis balls.'

'Ugh!' she says with a grimace.

'To babies? Dogs? or balls?' I say and we both smile.

'That life's not for me,' she says and her forehead creases. 'Remember that time the cotton bud got stuck in my nose … remember?'

'Yes, you were practically hysterical. The more frightened you were, the smaller that nostril became.'

'Until you had the brainwave to cover the other one and blow down. I can't imagine what having a baby would be like.' The very idea makes her visibly shudder.

'Enough said. The labour ward is not for you. Not now anyways. Who knows for the future?'

She throws me a look and is about to say something sarcastic but in a quick change of direction asks me instead, 'Did you get my note? I left it where I knew you'd find it. Beside the kettle.' The mischievous grin in her blue eyes lightens the dark shadows beneath them.

I nod. 'Yes, I got it. It brought me back.'

'You'll probably keep it,' Ellie says with a knowing look. 'Bet you still have all the ones I gave you,' she adds.

'Of course not,' I lie. There's one I *did* keep. The one she left me on her eighteenth birthday when she was leaving for her Debs. Her soft rosy lips kissed onto a paper napkin and the words *Don't wait up Ma!* still preserved in a small picture frame in a box of keepsakes in my wardrobe. Precious as her baby shoes. As is last night's note, though her lips are not so full, her words more a hurried scrawl. Maybe I should tell her how much these keepsakes mean to me. That I hold them and they give me comfort when the lump is too big for my throat.

Ellie pushes back from the table and begins clearing away our breakfast. The moment passes. Maybe it's just as well. Between the song and the note and the memories, I'd only cry, and crying isn't a good look.

'I'll take care of these, go back to bed for a while, it's still early,' I say, taking our bowls from her hands. Such small hands too.

'I thought we'd catch Bowie at the Brooklyn Museum,' she says, unable to hide her relief.

'I'm more an Ink Spots woman,' I say. 'We'll do something later.' Ellie looks at me as if I've gone crazy and shakes her head before heading towards her bedroom, Frankie at her heels. I turn away and move towards the kitchen. I begin to hum, filling up with the melody.

Foxes

DS Maolalai

may. early morning
and mist curls
like milk poured
in tea: a child
walking, their figure
in profile. a bag
on one shoulder
and a plastic toy.
wearing a uniform.
wearing pants
and black shoes.

through light fog
over one of those
green spaces
which appear
in new suburbs
between new
the construction,
the roundabouts
and short rows
of pharmacies.

a couple of swings
and a small apple tree
stand in emptiness.
sometimes at night
there are foxes.

a silhouette
with cold hands
in his pockets
and wet shoes.

Natural History

Jamie O'Halloran

In your shadow I learn whitethorn,
and hear the spade slicing turf.
Our shed is stacked with a half-trailer's
load, so we'll be warm through
winter.
                    The gestures of death –
snowdrop's bowed head, guard of honour
from church to graveside – create
a passage tomb of reckoning,

corridor where I will walk my grief
at the prospect of breath's last
casting, its shadow preserved
in remembering's bog.

Thoughts of Sunlight

Brigitte de Valk

CLOUDS FORM OVER MY MIND like silent heretics. The nature of their being here is uncertain. I worry for her health. A jug rests on the countertop. It is empty and cracked. Her mind is elsewhere. Two hands lie folded on her lap. I would like to say that I am being helpful, but really, I am just here. Standing next to a large window. Light filtering through glass.

Her palms quiver.

The ink is a tender navy, sinking deeply into her hands.

A vase of fake, white roses stand guard. Their petals are smothered in dust.

I can do nothing about her hands.

My grandmother rocks gently in her chair. A set of chimes dangle. They reflect and scatter pale light across the room. Crescents of water beguile her eyes. Shattered eggshell litters a tea tray. I often wonder at the scalp showing beneath her frayed hair.

'Thin air emotionally affects me,' she wrote, five months ago. This was the last sentence I could decipher. 'They are probably going to win.'

There is a timidity to the sky outside. It wallows palely. Cedar tree fronds shift in the air. The day has only just begun. A white slipper falls off my grandmother's foot. It is a plain thing. I should purchase her something more luxurious. The chimes tinkle, in time with my reaching down for the slipper. I place it back on her foot. It will probably slip off soon.

Three alternate emotions circle around my heart. I try not to feel them. There is nothing protecting us from the view outside. The drapes are being laundered.

Her pores are broken mouths, swallowing navy.

I can do nothing about her hands.

Birds create noise, soundlessly, on the other side of the glass. A dark echo of rain falls at the back of my mind. I glance at my grandmother. I hope that behind her closing lids, her recollections are a softened mass. The letters scrawled on her palms and over her knuckles are senseless. Inaccessible thoughts.

*

I fruitlessly search. There is a shape that I need to outline. It belongs partly to a face. Something soft and feminine, awash with focused intent. I am in monochrome. Unintentionally. My clothes all match. Black, battered classics line the shelves. Their pages have been thumbed by strangers. I peer at the used shoes clumped together in a box. Must and hope pervades this shop.

Sweat kisses my underarms. The old man behind the counter bites his lip. He too is looking for something.

*

Air greets me, sweetly. A memory of a warm body. There is an intricate pattern to the paving stones. Added to which, are a multitude of cracks. Clouds linger in the pale blue above. Concrete lies flatly beneath my feet. Summer is here. A woman labours over a watercolour in the square. People toss small glances at her as they pass by.

'I want the days to go away,' I overhear. I study a row of fountain pens, lined up in a window. Their bodies are bulbous, and their nibs are sharp. I could gift my grandmother a small bottle of fuchsia ink, but her palms would look desecrated. I bow my head. It's hard not to think about beauty. I must quiet my thoughts. I obscure the many outlines forming in my memory. The white bodies in the sky shift, and the window reflects too much light to look through.

*

Foam appears on the edges of her lips. I dab her mouth with a thin tissue. The white roses are doleful. My grandmother is ill at ease. Love appears cyclical today. I dip a teaspoon into an egg. The yolk is only a little congealed. I am becoming more accomplished at cooking her breakfast. Thin strips of toast lie on a side plate. A gossamer layer of butter glints on the bread, half-melted. The bone structure of her face is ovular.

She quails a little at swallowing. It requires a lot of her concentration. I evade the future. Glimpses of what may or may not occur do not interest me. An album of old photographs lies open on a bureau. My grandmother has had another visitor.

*

Navy desires of expression. A blooming of ink.

She emits a little gasp as I submerge her palms in a bowl of warm water. Clouds of weakened blue dishevel the transparent pool. I gently scrub at her aged skin. Her wedding ring sits on the side table; its dullened silver pockmarked and weary. I am careful to leave a few sentences, partially visible. I know that she will re-read her own words, and they will comfort her in a way that I cannot.

I pat her hands dry with a soft towel. Her nails are very wide. I push the ring back on her finger and lay her palms on her knees.

She looks at me.

Dim irises. Summertime is not a peaceful season. I feel so very uncertain. The mirror needs attention. It hangs lopsided. The leftover grease of fingertips mires its clear gaze. An answer permeates the air. My heart drums, carefully. The radiators are turned on high.

*

Heat scatters my attention. A warm body. My memory is dutiful. There is a possibility that I will not see him again. I walk across my room, naked. Scattered objects lie forgotten under my bed. A line of black socks hangs on my radiator. I take pleasure in the absence of clarity. I let my eyes drift shut, although it is morning. I feel the weight of light through my curtains. My chest rises and falls. Jackdaws serenade this moment.

The sky opens and shuts. It opens and shuts. I place a thin, cotton jumper in my bag. I am envious of children, so free to carry soft toys in their arms. I lock my door. Keys jangle. My bare skin tingles. My dress is almost weightless. The staircase unwinds itself slowly, no matter how quickly I descend. A thin man pauses as I pass. His frail hands clutch the railing. I wonder if it is all worth it, in the end.

*

'Dark raspberries, please.' Fruit looms above her. An earnest look is thrown over the counter. I stand in a queue. A phone call has been made. My heart beats a dire rose-thump. His voice was low. It always is. People shuffle forward. I could be anywhere. These faces are unrecognisable, but I know they are my neighbours. They must sleep close to me, cordoned off by walls during the quiet nights. I have dreamed of his clouds. The till beeps. He keeps them rolled up in a high shelf in his studio. His own private sky. They will be exhibited in a year. A brown paper bag is snatched from a bundle, hanging on the wall.

I would like to be stretched out like a cloud. All of my membranes dispersed; pulled apart. Lost in pale blue. Boundless. Unintentionally, I step on the heel of the woman in front. I quickly apologise. Yesterday, I scrolled through squares upon squares of clouds, neatly boxed. He is indeterminate. It is nearly my turn to pay.

*

'Thoughts of sunlight. Not actual sunlight.' The woman on the balcony shifts under a protective umbrella. I am sitting a few tables away from her. Our view is of the hot road below. Glass buildings glint at odd angles. A waiter places a tall glass of water in front of me. A frail, canary scarf is tied around the woman's neck. It flutters abstractedly. The city lies on its back, exposing its stomach to the sun. We have all submitted to its strength, apart from this woman, who resists, by clicking her tongue against the roof of her mouth. She listens intently to the voice on the other end of the line.

I look down. I would like his thoughts scattered amongst mine. It is indelicate to know so little of his mind. His paintings are beautiful geometrics. Trompe l'oeil, after trompe l'oeil. Each large sheet of paper hangs in perfect symmetry on his studio walls. His muse is indistinct. The persistent whirring of a fan bled into a calm white noise, the last time I was there. The fibres of a blanket were a little rough against my skin. I found traces of guttural calm in a dark backdrop, painted that day.

The rim of the cool glass touches my lips. Today, all clouds have been granted permission to leave the sky. Ice cubes rattle at the bottom of my drink. I was too honest. His face was close to mine. My feelings became apparent. The woman clinks her knife and fork together and lies them on her plate. She is nodding. Imprints of her lips linger on her napkin.

*

The night sky is thick with darkness. I watch it and wonder why hope blooms and dies, then blooms once more. A little black notebook is spreadeagled next to me. I have been jotting down bits of nothing. My words are careless and vacuous. I cannot define the sensations within. A circle of coffee remains at the bottom of my mug. My legs are bare. My knees are cool to the touch and nobbled. I trace the crescent of a scar. It was the first one I ever received as a child.

The universe of my dreams was hounded tonight. I procrastinate going back to sleep. I draw a template of life at the bottom of a page. I wonder if I could love with indifference. There is an innate timing, an invisible clock, to the inner-workings of affection. Over the streetlights, the dark softens to charcoal.

*

Reflections of navy, almost tangible.

I did not expect to see her today. The rules have been broken. The white roses are indignant. Someone has dusted them. A small radio in the corner plays static. I move to turn it off but my grandmother flinches. The chimes are perfectly still. Afternoon light berates the glass. I breathe a little deeper.

I balance many thoughts precariously in my mind, so that not one of them becomes dominant. My grandmother's mouth looks plum in the black and white photograph. Various shadows form to depict the scenery behind her.

Her hands are clasped. She is alone. The sky is graphite and old.

I put the picture down. My grandmother seems to watch me. I tend to her tea tray. Bone china rattles. Warm liquid spools in a saucer. Her wrists tremble as we lift the cup to her lips for the last time. I wish I could hear her voice again. She is beckoning for the pen. I unscrew its lid. The ink cartridge is running low.

The Philosopher of Water

Ciaran O'Rourke

Variations on poems and fragments by Friedrich Hölderlin (1770–1843)

My blood the flowing river, my poem the churning sky.
The words, you understand, were secondary.
Have you ever sung to an oak, an ash, the aspen's
shining leaves? Melodious trees, their shadows
carried me, bewildered, to the gate.
And then I heard the murmur –
the heartbeat of the gods.

~

My lament (for the dead) will never end: when our hill,
that dreaming green, is levelled, even ... our final
   daylight quenched.

~

The path parts, our way is lost, in loneliness, in grief.
This errant grief, a bitter stream, will lead me on
forever: it whispers from beyond the brink.

~

Late as I am, oh grant me,
breath, a single summer, or the first
autumnal chill restored, the lost, unhurried interval
with her, above the river, a stillness deep and green ...
   enough to fill my heart.

~

Blue to grey, the falling heights of heaven –
I walked below them slowly, pondering the past.
Sometimes, a sleepless god will weep,
a tide rise up between my ribs.

~

The morning clear, the air a vivid blue, once more
the dolphins fly, the island gannets dip,
the sun-quick waters raise, again,
an abundant harbour, tinkling:
the fishermen in motion,
the scintillating nets ...
whether memory or vision,
the bright sails lift my life.

~

A mist of sun on the wooden sill.
Within: a flush of plums, the knife
laid out, an idle bowl of bread.

~

I wanted only the dark light, caught,
in a fractal glass, the fragmentary
shadows stilled – and then to sleep,
drifting easy in the river of shades.

~

Bleak the mud, black the bark, the wind
a bitten rock! Oh where, in broken winter,
do the meadow-flowers rest, the lark
that lay between us (when we kissed)?

~

All that's left: relentless rain, spattering
    the steeples, clattering the slates.

~

The weight in the gut. The storm. The sting.
The loneliness unceasing. The greyest rain.
The earth itself a-brim, with bitterness,
with pain. All these, too, are lovely. We flare,
a little wick, before the darkness drops.

Margo

Triin Paja

I sing with the cemetery bird,
the thrush nightingale.
I make tea
with the cemetery weed,
the cowslip,
which I also gather
from the meadows of my life.
in such meadows
my father never held my hand.
someone places two slices of bread
on a grave.
should I pour vodka
on his grave, as some do?
my father ate pickles with his vodka.
he is not buried here.
I have never seen his grave
though I wander in his cemetery
with the flawless ferns
whose shadows he swallows.
I slip to steal a lilac branch.
I hang the dress of its scent
in my room.
I have thoughts

about dirt, if the smaller
the bones, the faster
the dirt's forgetting.
I refuse lucidity.
father-boy,
look at all the fruit
rotting towards your parched mouth
sweetening your name.

Crepe Myrtle

Susan Rich

I should have been a crepe myrtle, resistant to pests and disease —
should have been known by my nicknames: *Purple Magic, Ebony
Flame.*

I'd have lived as a popular resting spot for cardinals, larks, bluetits.
Could have been a pine siskin — an elegant flash of wing. Been a star

magnolia, close to extinction in the wild, child world —
sexy as a fragrant fringe cup drinking it up along riverbeds. A salmon-

berry. A lady fern. I should have kept the baby. All the best flowers,
single blooms. All the boy birds, yellow bellied sap suckers.

Could have nested in the cavity of a blue atlas; become a field
note, bilingual, old; fought romantic battles with stinging nettles —

avoided mildew and armoured scale. Now I night jasmine,
I honey suckle, I myrtle — requiring little water or microbial soil.

O Fruto dos Anjos

Anne Ryland

Swithering, we scoop up a single fruit.
You carry it home, a bolster under your arm.
Part-wrapped in tissue, beautifully ugly,

it has long outgrown fruit bowls. Reclining
on our table, moored now, its pitted skin
a mottled lime-green, with yellow islands.

Three days to mellow. At last, the ceremony
of cutting-sawing the fruit in equal halves –
a spillage of wrinkly black seeds, viscous,

teaspooned out. First sight of the slippery
pinkish-amber flesh. Peel, slice. White plates,
pastry forks to spear the fanned-out crescents.

We marvel at the angels fathoming its secrets
then steer through a quiet beginning,
faintly musky, to the exuberant buttery ending –

that time when every meal, every flavour shared
was a voyage – uncharted, hair-ruffling –
and we let ourselves coast, deft at the helm.

Moira

Shannon Savvas

LIGHT COMES CREEPING ACROSS the rooftops; a wanton cat of wakefulness slinking home after a night of dissolution. It comes through her window, pads softly up the duvet of lilac sprigs onto her face. There it settles emboldened by, careless of, the dried snail-like trails of acceptance on her cheeks.

Moira shakes off her exhaustion and gets out of bed.

It is this day which will change everything.

Last night, wired by tiredness, dreading the tomorrow now upon her, the solution had arrived fully formed, complete and undeniable, like a long-needed lover whispering in her ear, bringing clarity and courage, seducing her beliefs and morals and fears until they were discarded like a silly spinster's garments protecting her unvalued virtue.

She'd lain all night waiting for dawn to light a fuse in her sluggish veins. And it had come. Her resolve ignited. It hadn't been a fickle flirtation.

A sting of cold water sluices the sleepless night from her skin. She leaves Donald's cup of tea by his bedside table before he wakes and slips out to get dressed before he can drench her with the night's urine.

After today, her brother's raging body filled with frustration and his spirit fuelled by vitriol would no longer be her problem to bear.

Today she would solve everything. Damn the consequences. There never was going to be a good way out of this.

But she had work to do. Not much, true. She'd done the big jobs – windows, garden, woodwork last month, after Anna the Practice Nurse arranged a respite week in the residential home for Donald.

Go and have a bit of fun, Moira, she'd said. *Have a wee rest. Get away. Treat yourself.*

What in heaven's name did Anna think a sixty-year-old woman of limited means and no imagination would do for a bit of fun?

Well, at my age, I expect bungee jumping is out, Moira had said, straight-faced, to Anna. The nurse had given her a paper-sharp look, thin and barely visible. A look that said ungrateful woman, after all the strings I've had to pull to get your Bastard Brother a bed at Oakwood House and a dialysis slot in Margate's Renal Unit. To be fair, *Bastard Brother* was Moira's term not Anna's. But that was her secret name for Donald for more than forty years.

Before she can start on the finishing up chores, Donald rings the brass school bell that sits on his bedside table. She'd bought it when he first moved back, sick and broken after years in Africa. The bell, like letting him stay, had been another mistake.

In his bedroom, the stink of excrement burrows deep into Moira's nose and clings to the delicate mucosa lining her nasal passages. The smell of the pig wallowing in his sty travels down her Eustachian tubes and bounces off the back of her throat and seeps like an oil spill into her brain; she would smell it for the rest of the day.

'I've got the shits,' Donald says, leaning back on his pillows like an Ottoman pasha at leisure in his court.

When she'd driven over to Oakwood to collect Donald, she had asked if he'd been incontinent.

No, they said. *Not at all.* And from Sue Turner, the home's manager, *Your brother's an absolute charmer.*

Ibrahim, his named nurse for the week, said he wished all his other clients were as easy to be with. Donald had sent one of the cleaners out to buy the staff a glutton's tray of Cadbury's Roses. The nurses had been almost festive.

After beautiful Ibrahim, of the caramel skin and high-domed forehead, had bundled Donald with surprising care and solemnity into her Ford Fiesta, he had taken Moira's hand in farewell.

'May Allah's blessings – Peace be upon Him – keep you both well.'

Moira slipped the clutch into first and drove off.

'Fucking black bastard. Just because I worked on the Bisha Mine construction with the Canucks, Ibo thinks I'm his best friend. Jesus, if he knew how many Eritrean women we banged. Did them in job lots, dirt cheap.'

In the bathroom, she peels his pyjamas from his muscle-wasted buttocks, and with fistfuls of toilet paper swabs the thick tarry stools from the skin of his haggard scrotal sac. The back of her throat clams shut like a vice to block the bitter bile swilling up her gullet. She sits him on the shower stool and as she hoses him down, sings *Abide with Me* in her head to drown his complaints.

Moira towels his old man's body while he gasps for breath. She kneels to dry his spindled legs and bunioned feet crowned with keratin-crusted toes.

'Just my fucking luck,' Donald huffs between breaths. 'Finally got a woman kneeling but she's too ugly and too stupid to give a man what he really, really wants.'

The leer in her brother's voice brings her back to the brink of vomiting because she knows, if she offered, kinship notwithstanding, he'd accept what he'd demanded and taken when she'd been eleven years old. Moira rubs cream into his dry shins and cracked heels, a splinter of half-torn nail catches on the sleeve of her cardigan. Donald kicks her chest, knocking her off balance, her hip banging against the edge of the bath.

'Go easy, you stupid cunt.'

When she gets him back into a clean bed, he says, 'I need a piss.'

'Use your bottle.'

Donald fumbles under the bedcovers.

'I can't get my dick in the hole, for Christ's sake.'

That'll be a first, she thinks, then mentally slaps the thought down. Why is it only with him my head fills with filth? Filth she has never, ever said out loud. Filth she has learnt from Donald.

She snakes her hand under the sheets through the gap in his pyjama bottoms to guide his flaccid penis into the bottle. It gives a small jump, like the pulse of a tiny heart. She gags.

'Still got the touch, Moira. How long since you had a handful of dick?'

'You would know, Donald.'

'Sweet Jesus. That long? No wonder your mouth is tight as your arse.' He laughs and coughs before hoiking something wet and thick back up his nose and swallowing.

'Finished, Donald?'

He nods. She removes the bottle, taking care this time not to touch him.

'Feel free. Hand or mouth – as long as I keep my eyes closed, either would do the job for me.'

She really wants to punch the smirk off his face. But another few hours, then he won't be laughing.

'You're vile, Donald. Always was. Always will be.'

He chokes again on his laughter. 'At least I did you a favour. Christ Almighty, was I really the only man you ever had?'

'You weren't a man then and you're not much of one now.'

'What's made you so bloody gobby this morning?' He fists the bottle from her hand to the floor. 'When you've cleaned that make me some breakfast.'

Downstairs, Moira washes her mother's Royal Doulton figurines in warm soapy water and buffs them dry, bringing the gilded details to a sentimental brightness. As a girl, she'd complained every Saturday morning when her mother asked her to do that one chore. One last time. It is the least she can do.

After she's done the silver, she goes upstairs and peeps through the hinge crack of Donald's door – he is sleeping. She turns off his television, takes the remote from his hand, and downstairs in the kitchen she smashes it like a clove of garlic with the broad side of the meat cleaver.

Donald rings his bell as she drinks a final cup of tea.

Beneath its clamour, she whispers *GodforgivemeGodforgivemeGodforgiveme for the sin I am about to commit.*

'Where's my fucking remote!' The bell crashes against the closed bedroom door.

Moira calls Star Taxis and books the cab.

'Medway Hospital, love? Righto. Ten minutes. The driver will honk when he arrives, and it won't be because he loves Jesus.'

She hangs up on the man's easy laughter, removes her mother's rings, laying them in the cracked saucer on the kitchen sink windowsill. The one her mother used. It seems fitting.

Donald's profanities scream like a banshee down the stairs. He's made his stinking bed, let him lie in it, she thinks, pulling up her sleeve. She takes an elastic bandage, winds it from her fingers to her elbow and doubles a thick rubber band above the joint and unwinds the kitchen-sink tourniquet. Her arm blanches, zings with hypoxia. For a minute, she stares at her hand, flexing, extending the fingers. She will miss them. In the street, the taxi honks. Because she no longer believes in the love of Jesus, she lays her arm on the newspapers and towels, ready to soak up the blood.

Her left hand reaches for the meat cleaver.

Death Knocks

Niamh Twomey

like a nib on the rim of an inkwell, a ticking
clock or a farrier's knife scraping the mountain from a hoof.
I wake to the sound like a hook being hung
for an almanack. *Clack clack clack.*
Just a mother wren hunting for worms.
Or perhaps a hawk seeking shelter.
Maybe an old chaffinch, losing track of time.
Or a moth caught in a web, beating its wings
on the doorframe of its final hours.
I rise out of bed, open the door to the fluttering of heartbeats.
They enter me, your flock of winged messengers
come to keep watch through the dark months ahead.
In the morning I await my father's knock
to tell me you are dead.

Roundstone

Mark Granier

i.m. Barbara Nolan

Our best times together we were always on holiday
from ourselves. I heard you kept
something of your insouciance; in your last weeks
throwing a party at your house in the Allihies,
laughing as you told a friend how strange it was
to know you were dying and not
believe it. Remember our first play
at being lovers – a cottage with a loft bed
in the breathing thatch, the broad hearth
big enough for a child to stand in.
We'd stoop under the mantle into that
uncovered well-space framing
an airy rectangle of stars,
our faces lit by the clarity, rising towards it.

Snapdragons

Rachael Hegarty

Garden edging in Finglas – breeze blocks
painted white, filled with soil and flaming red
with late snapdragons. Da told me they roared
fire at night and kept our home from all harm.
Them blocks fell off the back of a lorry –
drivers took against the developer.
The paint came from the nixer man's secret stash.
Topsoil was a night-barrow and dash job.
Of course, I knew none of that craic back then.
All's I knew was what I was told and shown –
only the queen bee or a magic girl
knows how to charm open the dragon's mouth
with a daylight tickle of its petal jaws.
Then snapdragons will guard the gaff all night.

Sympathy for the Leaves

Kevin Higgins

Praise the thick roots of the tree:
who you are,
who you were,
who you will be.
That which you never see
and often forget,
rough days, keeps you standing here.
For not everything is planted
in the stone flecked earth
you stand in.

Pity the leaves,
those who know not
what throws them about
and out of the garden.
Their whispers
are not opinions
but what way the wind
is sending them just now.

Gemütlichkeit

Michael Lyle

Not known for rounded edges,
my German ancestors
yet created a word

for father's hand
on mother's shoulder
as she cooks,

mother's arms encircling his waist
as he washes dishes,

delicious dinner and laughter
at my childish jokes
family stories, bedtime book,
tucked in with a kiss,
a ripe stillness ...

whatever wars
the world wages
as yet beyond my ken,

this circle of certainty
evanescent as one touch.

Robins Don't Feed with Sparrows

Lourdes Mackey

A YEAR AGO TODAY Edith Elizabeth Webb died. She was only fifteen, but we will not forget her. Nothing she did was dull, not from the first moment we met her. Over the years we had glimpsed her – walking with her governess, riding her pony – but, until the beginning of last summer, we had never spoken to her. I was home from my first year at boarding school, the others just finishing seventh book with my father, who is schoolmaster in the village. I envied them – soon to throw away their satchels forever. It was a Sunday in early June, a day of long sunshine and sky blues, the air soft like a hand on your cheek. Monkey Sweeney and me were damming the narrow part of the stream at the end of 'The Big Meadow', layering and packing with stones, rocks, sticks, sods – anything we could cram in. Monkey was a tall hungry rake, quick with a sneer. In summer he regularly went barefoot and could walk on stones or stubble and never get any kind of cut. He liked animals better than he liked people. 'If he could,' his sister Aggie said, 'he'd marry a horse.' The girls had tagged along mainly because Kathleen Goggin had her eye on Monkey. She and the others were sitting on the bank, dipping their toes in the water, and chattering about some foolish thing when suddenly they went quiet. A strange roar could be heard, not like that of any animal, a roar with size to it, a roar that closed in louder and louder. Monkey and me jumped onto the bank and raced towards the meadow gate, the girls following in the useless way that girls run.

It turned into the avenue, raising dust that curled in the air and at first cloaked our vision. But when the dust settled there it was – slowly negotiating the bumps and troughs of the avenue – a De Dion Bouton four-seater. I recognised it immediately, I'd seen one in a magazine in the school library. It wasn't the first automobile in the parish – Doctor Twomey had a Ford, a Model T, a plain black box, dented and damaged from cutting corners and scraping off ditches. It spluttered and clattered and regularly backfired, frightening the life out of animals and people alike. One time it went mad and ran over four of Noreen Daly's chickens. The doctor didn't understand what the fuss was about, but as Mrs Daly said, 'How could he and him from a class that never had to count its chickens.' The De Dion Bouton was nothing like the Ford. it was shiny red, open topped, low on the ground, decked with fancy wheels and door handles – perfect. Miss Edith sat in front beside the driver. Behind, sat her mother and blanketed in beside Mrs Webb was the Major. As the automobile motored past, the Major suddenly jerked his head over the side and streaked the shiny red with green vomit. The Major, who according to my father was a hearty man that read Chesterton and drank pints, now looked grey and gaunt. The motor stopped. Mrs Webb didn't move, just sat there, like it had nothing to do with her, staring ahead with a queenly air. Miss Edith opened the passenger door, stepped off the running board and strode towards us. She stood a few feet away, in between us and the Major, who was still heaving but was now coming up empty. She spread her patent, buttoned boots slightly, taking better possession of the space. We all grew still staring at her – fitted from head to heel in bright yellow, her hair a mass of black curls.

'I'm Edith Elizabeth Webb', she said, in a voice strong and sweet like golden syrup. 'My father isn't well.' She heaved a sigh. 'He is a hero, home from the war.' With grown-up confidence she looked from one of us to the next. Our faces were burned from summer sunshine, hers was winter white. The girls stared at their toes, so dumbstruck that when a bee started buzzing around, they forgot to start up their usual screechy racket. Monkey stood like something had taken him over. He flushed up – that and his scutch of foxy hair giving him the look of a rhubarb stick. He gazed at Miss Edith like he could do it all day. The Major was coming back to himself and so she turned and waved goodbye, her arm held high as she stepped onto the running board. 'See you soon,' she called. We stared after the automobile until the bend in the avenue shut it from view. Then Kathleen, who always carried on like she was the cat's meow, led the girls in a fit of giggles. '*I'm Edith Elizabeth Webb,*' she mimicked, '*yah and I'm Queen Mary.*'

The following Saturday morning and every Saturday after that, as punctual as the church bell, the Dion Bouton drove out through the lodge-gates and turned left towards town. Then Miss Edith joined us. She stripped to her bloomers and swam in the lake amid loud tuts from the girls, who had suddenly gone all holy. Monkey taught her to sling-shoot and lay a snare and they regularly disappeared into the wood together. During the week she helped Aggie bring tea from the kitchen to where we were thinning turnips or fruit picking. She often joined in, her hands becoming scratched, her skin losing its winter pastiness. She was soon as good as any of us at driving cattle and blocking a gap and could manage the horse-rake or turn the hay. She shortened the work with stories about her school in England and about herself and her father. She told us the story of Pollyanna and 'the Glad Game', lifting us up with sentences that described timber houses and snowy fields. Monkey hacked her name under his in the bark of the old chestnut tree.

Mrs Webb sent a card inviting my mother and me to afternoon tea. This was a surprise, for in the past – before the Major went to war – only my parents were invited to sit in Willowgrove House and discuss important matters. But the words were clear: 'There is no need for the schoolmaster to accompany you as the Major is indisposed.' Without my father, my mother worried that she might be a bit lost and practised things to say in case of awkward silences. She need not have bothered, attempts at conversation bounced off Mrs Webb. She threw out questions that she didn't want answered, like 'Wasn't life wonderful when servants were silent and grateful for their jobs, and before anyone heard of Sinn Féin?' She nodded at anything my mother said, her gaze sliding past on its way to the clock. We sat on uncomfortable high-backed chairs while Aggie laid four china, gold-rimmed cups on a low table. Mrs Webb looked at me and said, 'I understand that you are friends with Aggie's brother.' I nodded. 'A blackguard, I hear,' she said. I swallowed and stared at the rows of polished silver on the heavy sideboard. Miss Edith, who was sitting beside me, began fiddling with her skirt. After the tea – that my mother later said was 'too long wet' – Mrs Webb walked us into the hall. 'And you're sure you won't have a sherry,' she said, as she led us to the door.

June turned to July and Monkey and Miss Edith spent every spare moment together. They walked the paddock and sat on the low grass beside the wild nasturtiums. Aggie found them in the walled orchard when she went to pick gooseberries. One Saturday when we were testing out the raft,

Kathleen Goggin spied them holding hands under the canopy of rhododendrons on the far side of the lake. 'That fella is getting above himself,' she snorted, 'now he thinks he's a big shot.' Then she called Miss Edith a slut, though none of us knew exactly what that word meant. Monkey gave Miss Edith a hazel rod and when we were fishing took her off to show her where the otters feed. Aggie warned him that the Mistress was asking questions and that if he didn't stop, he wouldn't be kept on as farmhand after the summer-work. I tried to explain that sitting in the rose garden, in plain sight of the dining-room window, went against the grain – but he didn't listen.

Early one Saturday, him and me were up on the galvanised roof of their cottage trying to repair the leaks, something that his father kept promising to do, but didn't. 'That useless caday,' my mother said. 'More in his line to mind his care, save below in Canavan's pub too far gone in porter to do a hand's turn.' Mrs Sweeney had the reputation of a saint. Lately, she'd been finding extra milk and eggs on her windowsill and sometimes flowers to cheer her up. 'Mrs Webb's special roses,' Aggie whispered, 'her Queen Anne's, ones she'd devoted herself to, heart and soul.' That Saturday morning, instead of turning left at the lodge gates, the De Dion Bouton turned right, drove up and stopped directly below us. Mrs Webb got out, looked up at Monkey and stood for a moment like she didn't know what to do with her rage. 'The company keeping will stop', she hollered and then an angry torrent, like released water, burst out of her. The gist of it was that 'robins don't feed with sparrows'.

Miss Edith didn't appear that day or any other. 'She's under lock and key,' Aggie said. 'Her mother is watching her like a hawk after a field mouse.' When Monkey tried to sneak inside Willowgrove House, Mrs Webb ran him. The Major was coming back to himself but against that the sickness was spreading faster than Doctor Twomey's Ford could travel. On our way back from mass on Assumption Day we saw that the De Dion Bouton was parked at Madge Healy's and watched it drive her up the avenue to Willowgrove House. It was Madge's job to bring someone into the world and send someone out. She laid Miss Edith on a long table in the little chapel with the artist's windows. The summer had been unusual, dry for weeks until that day when Miss Edith was shouldered out, then it poured. They buried her in the Protestant churchyard under a stone with names going back to the plantation of Munster. We all stood in a sodden, murmuring huddle at the gate – to set foot inside would draw the priest on us. The girls cried;

Monkey's face was waxen.

Monkey took to the bed and wouldn't get up, not even for my father. Aggie pleaded with him to take the farmhand job on offer at Willowgrove but that provoked such ire in him that Mrs Sweeney told her to leave it.

A fortnight later I returned to boarding school. My mother 's letters kept me up to date: 'Monkey was on an entirely different circuit – up half the night and in bed half the day.' Then she wrote that he had lied about his age and joined the brigade. This wasn't a surprise because, until Miss Edith, Monkey had always referred to Protestants as 'that crowd'. It was easy to see him high up on a lorry, a rifle across his back, burning barracks. Then, like a fox in the shadows, he was on the run.

A year has passed. Today, Assumption Day, walking by the Protestant churchyard on our way to mass, my mother suddenly stops and points in at Miss Edith's grave. There amongst Mrs Webb's festoon of roses and dahlias is a hazel rod enfolded by the biggest posy of wild nasturtiums that we have ever seen. My mother squeezes my arm and as we continue on to our own church, I think again, 'Robins don't feed with sparrows'.

have you ever noticed how swans

Laura McKee

---

glide in to land
wide winged
and now
I'm wondering about this

because land on water seems odd
that would be an island
but yes
all wide winged knowing

until their unexpected feet
hit water
start to run
across the surface

not like they're thinking
look I am jesus
more like their heads are going
oh fuck oh fuck oh fuck

I can't do this
I can't keep up
with myself
whatever

was I thinking
and then the next thing
no feet at all
like nothing happened.

After Effects

Karen J McDonnell

I put my wound to bed
settling back
revelling in home.

Drifted, pillowed on meds:
and there we were
arm in arm, companionable

like two old characters from Beckett.

That silent walk sparked in us
a flowing, an enveloping aura of
all that we once were.

You said, Come into the house.
We stood, tight together, before
the squad of astonished faces

and I was sure of you then.

Darling, I didn't need the morphine
to know yes, we once were,
and yes, it was a strange, clarified love.

Inishbofin Gauntlet

Alan McMonagle

for Elaine Feeney and Vahni Anthony Capildeo

Because the poets threw it down
and knew I wouldn't sleep, wanted to drift
awhile, be quickly lost in the mist shroud
until all I could hear was the corncrake sniggering
at my useless attempts to find a way
back to the sun-porch where earlier
the guitarman sang about the small fires
we don't mind owning up to and the cartoonist
told of the wallet-heavy coat Beckett draped
over a *clochard* in the Paris dark before quenching
the word-thirsty hoards and the song progressed
onto the big fires that send us curling guilty
under a bed in some long-forgotten room
which is possibly why we ended up drinking
beer called Mass until the actress revved
the sun-porch crowd for an hour-long rendition
of Bohemian Rhapsody that the writers mistook
for an invitation to do the dead-man's float,
scatter themselves into an island night ready
to wrap them in its soft bandage.

Pastoral Care

Katherine Meehan

You were the prom dress with no body in it,
thumbing the air at the county line,
near the banks of the wide red river.
No field was looking out
for you, no shepherd stepped
from the labyrinth of the corn —
not the monstrous American
robin, its freakish stride upon
the leaf mould, nor the cows;
on the nights their calves are taken,
they think only of themselves.
No home for you — roads only.
Life is a golden pickup truck, you said,
as golden as a hay bale, heated up
from the core, liable to combust —
oh darlin! You were the love-song
hitched to the tree frogs' ·chatter,
consort of the unpaved trailer park —
joyriding the fog beyond the chicken
yard, you were the mist that sighs
upon the windshield glass,
the midnight voice, crackling
with lust, the cosmic pulse
amidst the radio static —
when even the power lines
had turned their backs.

An Empire of Lies

Steve Wade

THE FIRST JIM ROGERS HEARD OF IT was the previous January. Sitting on the couch, with a full belly, while Garfunkel purred on his lap, the report came on the evening news. Like it was for so many others, this virus the media spoke about seemed remote, distant. Something that might as well belong to fiction and fantasy.

But, in the most classical fashion of life imitating art, the world quickly resembled something that had leaked from the pages of a science fiction novel. Schools and businesses were ordered to close their doors, movement and travel restrictions were imposed, social distancing was introduced, extended families were separated from each other, and the unwell and the infirm suffered without the reassuring touch of loved ones, the dying died confused and alone, and the dead, likewise, were unceremoniously laid to rest.

A naysayer to begin with, Jim Rogers regarded it all as an empire of lies – fake reports, exaggerated statistics, just another way of controlling the masses. His outlook faltered then switched during the second wave that had been predicted. Cases multiplied and the daily death rate rocketed, and even greater restrictions were put into place than those that had been gradually lifted.

Jim Rogers now went to the other extreme, his approach Darwinian. Here was a crisis from only which the fittest would survive. Straight away, he set about employing his skillset as an engineer and background as a builder to construct a bunker, a fully equipped shelter in the back garden of his home.

With a wife who had long ago left him for someone she felt was more important, and a grown son she had turned against him, he often pondered his existence. What was he for? The only ones Rogers had to look out for were himself and Garfunkel, his ginger cat and constant companion.

But, pandemic or no pandemic, he just got on with it. Kept himself busy with building projects.

'Another idiot standing too close,' a man in his sixties said to his wife about Rogers at the deli counter in his local supermarket.

'Thanks for that,' Rogers said aloud, which was enough to spark the man into an expletive-filled tirade.

The urge to retaliate, to point out that he'd been in line first, he resisted. He considered himself too old and ugly to know that trying to argue with inherent stupidity was fatuous.

When he had, on another occasion, asked the tattooed clown standing too close to him in a queue for the pharmacy to give him some space, the guy had deliberately coughed into his face and walked away. This moron, someone he knew to see from his own neighbourhood, had a shaved head full of tattoos. His hands too and his forearms were tattooed, so that it was his pallid face that looked fake. A small boy, his head dropped to his chest, trailed after him. The child was dark haired, the same haircut Jim Rogers' boy, Allen, had when he was that age, four or five. And the way he toddled along, talking to himself, he could have been his son's doppelgänger, or the boy reincarnated.

But all the issues and inconveniencies that arose from the global pandemic were as nothing when compared with the subsequent global calamities that ensued. As though horror and terror had come together in a deadly pair bond and produced offspring, the Bubonic and Pneumonic plagues broke out and spread across the globe. As the scientists and the medics extended their battle to find yet more vaccines, one of the most dreaded and anticipated of all mankind's fears came to pass. What began as the disgruntlement of the petty-minded leader of the world's second superpower at losing a conflict he had instigated led to the onset of an all-out nuclear war.

By then, Jim Rogers had constructed a liveable structure beneath the earth in his garden. With its own generator to run electricity, and a heat-controlled garden with halogen lights to grow vegetables, along with his stockpile of tinned meats and fish, pickled fruit, and cat food, he followed the media reports of the nuclear explosions and their aftermath. The smoke left behind by the attacks quickly lowered global temperatures by eight degrees. Experts predicted widespread famine. Producing enough food to sustain the global population, they said, would be almost impossible. They were right.

Reports from around the world included film footage of mass looting of shops closed under lockdown. And the looters, many now wearing gas masks and hazmat suits, didn't confine their looting to shops and businesses. Homes deserted by owners who had fled to places they considered safer were likewise targeted. But things got worse. The subsequent weeks brought reports of citizens attacking the homes of other citizens.

'It won't be long,' Rogers said to Garfunkel purring in his lap. The cat twisted his head and opened its eyes luxuriously. 'We'll have to be careful. They'll be here soon.'

And they came.

With CCTV cameras installed in his four-bedroomed cottage, Rogers watched helplessly, from his screens underground, a bunch of scrawny adolescents break into his home. Most, incredibly, without masks. His immediate impulse was to pick up his assault rifle, burst out of his bunker and take them out. He stopped himself. What if there were others about? He seldom came out of his shelter in daylight anymore, lest someone spotted him and discovered his concealed entrance beneath the floor of the old glasshouse.

His instincts were right. As though responding to some unknown summoning, other scavengers arrived.

Rogers witnessed the images of the hungry hordes that came soon after, each group more crazed and desperate than the last. One individual he recognised as the tattooed punk from the pharmacy. And this clown had brought with him his son. The boy was emaciated.

No choice had Rogers than to watch as the hordes ransacked the rest of the house. They tore the doors off cupboards, smashed plates and cups, ripped up carpets, broke tiles, pulled down bookshelves and squabbled together over any morsel they considered edible, from a packet of uncooked and years out of date noodles, to coffee sachets.

Inasmuch as the limited space in his bunker refuge allowed, Rogers, like a lion in a nineteenth-century zoo, paced back and forth.

'Sorry,' he said to Garfunkel when the cat bolted again from the computer room, terrified by Rogers' act of violence – kicking over a chair. 'Anyway, I'm off to have a bath.'

Garfunkel made a high gurgling note in his throat.

'Good puss.'

Once he had soaped himself and washed his hair, Rogers dunked his entire body below the water. He then lay back, his hands hanging over the edges of the bathtub, and let himself sink into exhaustion, the lavender scent of the bodywash carrying him back to a past that was only a fainter present –

yet a million miles away.

Jim Rogers awoke from a sleep he hadn't realised he'd fallen into. The water had turned lukewarm and his fingertips, like a cadaver's, were white and shrivelled. But when he twisted the hot tap in the bath, a trickle of icy water emerged. And then nothing.

'Shit,' he said, working his way out of the bathtub and to the sink. He twisted the taps, which coughed and spluttered for a bit before giving up. The booster pump, where he had teed-off the main water supply, had probably stopped working.

A quick check on the monitors and he saw that two or three of the marauders had jungled down on the floors in his house. In a couple of the rooms, they had open fires burning at the rooms' centres.

Shaking his head, which he enveloped in his hands, he closed his eyes, knowing, without yet considering the odds, that he was going to do something terribly risky. He never was someone to procrastinate.

Mid-winter now, he dug out a pair of long-johns, extra thick work-socks, a heavy fleece and a pair of boots. The fleece he pulled on over his protective suit. And with his gas mask in place, he put on a Russian bombers guard hat.

A stillson pipe wrench, an adjustable spanner, a hacksaw and other tools he individually wrapped in cloth as a way of preventing them from clanging together in his rucksack. Into a pocket, he put a roll of heavy-duty industrial tape. His rifle he hung about his neck.

Jim Rogers stood at the top of the steps beneath the door from his bunker that opened into the glasshouse and listened. With his back pressed to the door, he opened it. The blackness of night-time, along with the penetrating cold, creeped over him. Then something soft and ginger brushed against his leg and flashed past him. He followed it with the beam of his flashlight.

'Garfunkel,' he said. But he quickly readjusted to the cautious approach of a man in danger of being imminently under siege. He froze and cast about him with his flashlight and with his senses.

Priorities. Water. Without running water, he couldn't survive. He carefully made his way to where he had hidden the booster pump behind a snarl of brambles. His speculation was right. Switching off his flashlight so as not to draw unwanted attention or give away the pump's location, he tinkered around with it by touch until he got it working. Now he had to find Garfunkel before someone else did.

Not until he was a good distance from the hidden water pump did he switch on his flashlight. He then made the noises he used to call the cat, though in a subdued manner.

Garfunkel mewingly answered him. But when the beam he pointed in the cat's direction caught the animal's eyes, it darted towards the front of the house and disappeared inside through the cat-flap.

'Goddamn it,' he said.

He gathered himself and wasted no time in following it. Before entering his house, he placed his rucksack in the porch. Using the industrial tape, he attached the flashlight to the rifle's barrel. The rifle's safety switch he then clicked off.

Inside the house was a sulphuric hum of choking smoke – whatever these clowns were burning.

In the living room, there were three bodies sprawled out on the floor. Hesitant to approach them, he held his rifle at waist level. The light beam he rested on each of them long enough to gather they weren't breathing. None of their chests rose or fell. Poisoned. By gas or something. He had to move fast.

'Garfunkel,' he called, as he shifted the beam about the room.

That's when he heard something, a groan coming from his own bedroom. The door was already open. He stepped inside. There, on his mattress-less bed, was a figure he instantly recognised. The tattooed punk from the pharmacy.

'Hey,' he said, not knowing what he was going to do. 'Hey you.'

Nothing. He moved closer and nudged the body with the rifle barrel. No indication of life. No more coughing into the faces of strangers for this guy, he thought. But then that groaning sound again. It was coming from the wardrobe. He opened it. Nestled in the shirts and sheets on the wardrobe floor, the boy. His sleeping face could have been the face of his own son, as though he'd fallen into a coma twenty years ago.

Putting the safety catch back on his rifle, Jim Rogers leaned into the wardrobe and picked up the boy. Gently, he used a T-shirt, which he wrapped about the boy's nose and mouth. The child stirred.

'I have you. You'll be okay.'

Carefully but quickly, he made his way out of the house and back to the bunker. With the boy safely laid out on his mattress, Jim Rogers now knew exactly what he was for.

In Spate

Geraldine Mitchell

There are no river gods, whatever you've been told.
No goddess either. The mudded waters lost their faith

before faith was, missed their footing, plunged down
gravity's sheer ladder from bee-sipped hills to heartless

ocean, swelled from one-ply thread to flailing hawser,
from feeble dribbles moon-bright on some far-off slope

to this, a murderous herd dull with dirt, locked in some
feral madness, condemned to a neck-long, back-long rage

of self-annihilation. This river will not see you light a
candle on the bridge. The flowers you throw will waltz

a moment, then be gone. The river knows no gods.
Appease it now.

Incubation

Peggy McCarthy

By a roadside verge in drenched grass
a blob of jellied spawn shivers in the wind.
Glenmalure's gullies gush and spill
the valley soaked in spring rain.
Gorse swells yellow from dripping ditches
deer on the uplands, their antlers prong the sky
like ancient herds through granite-flecked hills.
Clinging by the hard shoulder, pinpricks of life
thicken at my feet. Underneath, the squelch of clay
margins rutted in tyre tracks
wheels slice past a shudder away –
not yet time to start counting frogs.

When We Are Loved Enough, Then Peace Comes

Marie Marchand

I whisper improvised poems
along your drought-riddled skin.
You lay in the quiet, thirsty for
any drip of kindness

left in words.
You have longed for such tenderness
to return, to quench you

at dusk.
You miss your mother's lullabies,
how her exhalations mingled with prayers

like sunlight on a river.
The world threw its cloak over your ears.
Almost forgotten is the honeyed flow,
the rhythm and timbre of words

when spoken with love.
The echo is not completely lost.
There remains a vibratory presence

that pervades your cells with

enfoldments of belonging.
You drink from the cusp of language
under the tent of my breath and it
all comes back:

this, feeling loved.
And you remember enough
to heal.

We've Probably Missed the Waving

Antoinette McCarthy

THERE'S A CRACK IN THE CEILING. A pair of faded blue and white deck-chair striped curtains at the window. A St Brigid's cross hanging on a nail on the wall. She feels sick, her head throbs. The wedding. The house Sean found through a relative of the groom. The morning after. She turns her head on the pillow. She is alone in the bed.

It's raining, a dull grey light. It could be any time of day. Sinead gets up slowly. She needs water, painkillers. She walks down an orange-tiled hall, finds her handbag by the front door. There's a dining room with a large picture window. Rivers of rain run down the glass. It looks as if all the world outside is dissolving.

Just beyond the dining room is the kitchen. She fills a glass from the tap, feeling the tablets scrape the sides of her throat as they go down. Back in the dining room she sits at the table, facing the window. The rain has eased a little and there, just over a little wall with the paint chipped at the lip, is a lake. She lets her eyes rest on the dirty expanse of water, choppy under a low, grey sky and waits for the codeine to kick in. Maybe it's just the disorientation of waking alone in a strange house but she feels unnerved as if something important has happened, but she can't remember what it is.

A blustery wind has picked up, the sun breaking through the cloud. In a pool of light, right out on the lake, two figures are standing on a bit of rock. She gets up quickly, steadies herself against the table as she inches to the window. There's no boat, just two people, stranded, in the middle of the deep water.

'Oh shit,' she says, 'where's Sean?'

She walks back out to the hall, she needs to find the sitting room, a sofa. The sofa is where Sean sleeps these days, even at home. Out of choice, out of an aversion to sharing their bed or out of a sleep that can only come when he's lying there, watching TV and pretending that he doesn't want it at all.

Sean is fully clothed, asleep, half his face pressed into a brown velvet cushion. His shirt has ridden up revealing a straggle of hair down to his belly button and a ridge of pale fat that is folded over the waistband of his hired suit trousers.

'Sean.' Her voice comes out like a growl. Nothing. She clears her throat and tries again, louder, 'Sean.'

She watches the sound flicker across his eyelids. He turns over, revealing a cheek scored with red creases.

'There are two people stranded out on the lake, Sean.'

Sean rolls himself off the couch, tasting the inside of his mouth with a sticky slap.

'What?' he says and stumbles off, going to the dining room, passing the big picture window to get to the kitchen.

'Look.'

But Sean raises a hand above his head and keeps moving.

She waits at the window, listening to the tap running, listening to him gulping, watching the two out in the middle of the lake.

'There,' she says.

'Are you sure?' He is slowly scanning the view. 'I see them,' he says, and she feels a strange sense of relief that he can see them too. 'How did they get out there?'

'Maybe they pulled the boat up and didn't tie it properly.'

'Or maybe,' he says, searching for an idea to throw into the pot, 'the boat capsized and they had to swim for it.'

'What should we do? Ring someone?'

'Who would we ring?'

'The guards? Or the coastguards?'

'We're fifty or sixty miles from the coast, Sinead. Anyway, there are loads of houses looking out onto the lake. Someone will have been up before us. Someone will have rung already.'

She looks at him. She is shocked by his easy confidence that somebody else had already shouldered the task. She feels the blood rushing from her head. Sits down. She hates the way he looks at these people in need and the way it brings her to a standstill.

'What we need is tea.' Sean rubs his hands together. 'I'll go find a kettle.'

After a minute she follows him out to the kitchen. He's all business now; collecting mugs, milk and sugar. She fills the teapot, takes it out to Sean who is seated at the table, facing the window, looking out.

'Are they still there?' she says, as she pours.

'Well, they're not going anywhere.'

They are a long way off, such a tiny bit of rock, so much water.

'They don't seem to be waving,' she says.

'We've probably missed the waving,' says Sean, as if she's trying to start an argument.

He gets up and goes back down the hall.

She doesn't want to watch the two stranded souls, out there, sitting here on her own. She puts her head down, thinks of the wedding, of them all sat at their breakfast in the hotel. Sean had said he could do without it, the morning after, the same faces with the hangovers and without the goodwill. Locked together in their struggle to get through platefuls of salt and fat. He made a few phone calls and found this place. She hears a toilet flush.

'That's the last of the weddings anyhow,' she says as he sits down. There was a time that would have been a hint and later perhaps a dig but today, she realises, it's just a fact.

He takes a large slurp of tea. 'Mairead was really going for it. She was like someone let out.'

Mairead had trailed around after Sinead in college. She was all doughy and unformed with none of the sharp, shiny edges that Sinead was busy crafting for herself. Hovering in doorways, that was Mairead. While she and Sean were always in the centre of the room.

Mairead was married now with two kids and at the wedding wearing a pink satin dress that caressed the soft swell of her stomach. Two glasses of champagne and she was giggling like a schoolgirl and falling against a tall husband who held her with a casually protective air. Sinead pushes herself away from the table.

'I'm going to the toilet,' she says, 'tell me if anything happens.'

Mairead had cornered her again at the afters, gabbled on, domestic details, pregnancy and birth. Sinead had looked down at the most expensive pair of shoes she'd ever owned and tried to let the stories wash over her. Mairead and her sticky-handed toddler clinging to the back of her knee.

Mairead and her infant clamped to her breast for hours on end.

'We have a bottle of champagne every Friday,' she'd said, 'just to celebrate.'

Sinead catches sight of herself in the mirror above the sink. The thin lines that have appeared around her mouth. The greying, puffy bags under her eyes. She crosses her arms, rubbing her hands briskly up and down, from her shoulder to her elbow. As if she's trying to stay warm.

Sean hasn't moved. She sits beside him. They drink tea until the pot is empty.

She used to ask him what he was thinking. It seems like a ridiculous thing to say now. In ten years, they've learned how to negotiate around each other. Lines have been drawn. Their lives running smoothly in the spaces in between. And they get on. They have always got on.

'You didn't get to bed,' she says.

'It must be a local sport.'

'What?'

'Standing out on the lake.'

Yesterday he had been in his element, holding court, had them all in stitches. It had made her want to scream, 'Enjoy him, this is the best of him!'

'No one has come for them,' she says.

The one on the left shuffles. From cold maybe. Or from standing still for such a long time.

Mairead's toddler hand in hers, her infant on her breast, her husband's arm around her waist. Mairead being touched, that's what it was all about, endless accounts of how Mairead was, is and has been touched. You could see it on her face. You could hear it in her voice.

Where on Sinead's face is it written? Is it etched into the thin lines that are crawling their way out from her lips? Is it nestled in the bags under her eyes? The tell-tale signs that she goes for months at a time and is never touched. At all.

They had both been looking forward to the wedding. It had been years since they'd all been together. But while Sean had slipped straight back in, as if he was sliding into a warm bath, Sinead had found herself at the edges, spotting bald patches and noticing who had a bit of middle-age thickening setting in. It made her feel mean, judgemental. She had gone to the bar. Got caught in a conversation with somebody's aunt who took her through a messy hysterectomy and the years of fallout after. She could hear Sean laughing.

Sinead looks at Sean. At his big old curly head. His mouth is open slightly, the way it always is when he is relaxed, making him look like a child. He's gentle and funny but he doesn't want to touch her. And she doesn't want to touch him.

She goes to stand at the window, leans her head against the cold pane.

'Why don't they do something? Jump up and down, swim for it, something. Why are they just standing there? What are they waiting for?'

'Here we go,' says Sean, and he comes to the window. He points to a boat that has just rounded the headland. The man in the boat is facing the island, heading straight for the rock.

'Come on.' Sean is urging the boat on like it's about to score.

As the boat travels across the lake, travels across the large picture window, she can see how much Sean needs this, the rescue, the happy ending. It's what they've both been sitting here waiting for.

'What?' he says.

She looks out to the lake. The boat is too big. The two people on the island are dwarfed by it. And they are not looking to their saviour they are still facing the two watching at the window. As the boat putters on by, two birds that have rested a while on a rock, out on the lake, take flight.

Sean is laughing.

'Birds, Sinead, they're birds.

Sinead is watching the birds, cormorants she thinks, as they fly low over the lake, away from them.

'Come on, show's over,' Sean says over his shoulder as he goes out into the kitchen. 'I think they left us some rashers in the fridge.'

The birds part company.

'I want to be desired,' she calls out to him.

'What?' he says. 'Enough birdwatching.'

Sinead is tracking one of the birds now. Its clear, sure progress. It reaches the opposite shore of the lake.

'I want to caress someone until they tingle and shiver,' she says.

'Sinead, I'm starving, and I can't hear you.'

The bird is heading for a patch of blue sky.

'I want to be touched until I can't cope with it anymore,' she whispers, and smiles.

A patch of blue that shows the day holds promise.

The Crannóg Questionnaire

Elizabeth Reapy

How would you introduce yourself as a writer to those who may not know you?

I'm a fiction writer primarily but during the past few years I've been dabbling in other areas. Currently I'm completing a feature-length screenplay and have also finished a handful of therapeutic sleeping aids picture books for small children. I'm really interested in understanding the energy and workings of the creative process too and enjoy collaboration with other writers and artists.

When did you start writing?

I don't remember a time not knowing that I wanted to write. This has been with me from a very young age. Stories – reading and writing them – were my main preoccupation for most of my life. When I was 22 I began a Master's in Creative Writing in Queen's and after that, I worked to professionalise my passion.

Do you have a writing routine?

Not really at the moment. I spent a lot of my twenties practising discipline and focus and finding different ways to be productive but now I'm much more relaxed. I know what needs to be done will be done and can trust that I have that in place. I anchor my days with a sea swim in the morning and a gym class at some point in the day. These are indirectly part of my writing routine as they ground me for the imaginary and cerebral parts of writing. They also balance that isolating physical act of sitting at a desk for hours too with community, embodiment and nature.

When you write, do you picture somehow a potential audience or do you just write?

The audience I pictured in the past was usually an earlier version of me who would have benefited from what I was sharing. Now, as I've explored a lot of my trauma and anxieties in depths and don't feel as compelled to use them as creative fuel, the main audience I write for is the people who would connect to what I am expressing.

I do also just write – journalling or morning pages, etc. – but that writing is for me, as there are different conventions and considerations to be in place when it's for external readers and people who aren't privy to my mind's eye and preoccupations.

Frequently, something is sparked here in these motley rambles that can be translated and transformed into something that has potential for a reader.

Some writers describe themselves as planners, while others plunge right in to the writing. Would you consider yourself a planner or a plunger?

I'm probably both and I'm finding a lot of projects have different rhythms for how they unfold.

Plunging in, when it all starts flowing, is probably the most enjoyable way to work but having an outline – a map – is useful, even if it's to deviate from it. It can break down the task into smaller steps which I sometimes need too to motivate me to start. Once I'm in, the momentum usually takes care of itself.

How important are names to you in your books? Do you choose the names based on liking the way they sound or for the meaning? Do you have any name-choosing resources you recommend?

They are important. Sometimes they'll come to me and be the only thing I have to start with and I have to figure out what the story is, based on this title or character.

It can be intuitive too. I brainstorm lists of names and then if one or a few of them glint, I'll go down the rabbit hole with them, see what comes up from researching them.

Is there a certain type of scene that's harder for you to write than others? Love? Action? Erotic?
I'm not really good with measurements or distances, things like that. So I have a bit of a struggle with spatial, mathematical or mechanical descriptions and would have to do a good bit of figuring out how to write these into scenes.

Tell us a bit about your non-literary work experience, please.
I'm a qualified secondary school teacher but I wasn't able to write when I was teaching, my creative and emotional energy was used up, so I left it. I've worked in a lot of different places – pubs, hotels, restaurants, factories, shops, offices – all while trying to fund my writing.
Ironically, since becoming a professional writer, I tried to move away from it altogether and trained in fitness instruction and also as a hypnotherapist amongst other healing modalities. I have a deep interest in health and wellbeing, with a particular emphasis on the power of mindset for living happily.
I often combine these worlds, writing bespoke scripts for clients and also bringing therapeutic and physical resources to my creative writing and mentoring practices.

What do you like to read in your free time?
For the past few years, my reading has mostly been non-fiction – creative, spiritual or psychological texts. It has felt more pressing for me to understand as much as I could about the psyche, emotions, trauma, mind and the unconscious and I've gone to fairly esoteric places in my studies.
I am slowly returning to novels and story collections and beginning to read poetry again.

What one book do you wish you had written?
There are so many, for many different reasons. *Matilda* by Roald Dahl is coming to mind, or *The Catcher in the Rye* by J.D. Salinger, *Animal Farm* by George Orwell, *Self-Help* by Lorrie Moore, *Olive Kitteridge* by

Elizabeth Strout, *The Commitments* by Roddy Doyle, *The Cartographer Tries to Map a Way to Zion* by Kei Miller or *Jesus' Son* by Denis Johnson. These are all books that blew my mind reading them for the first time and still give me a thrill when I revisit.

Do you see writing short stories as practice for writing novels?
It depends on the writer. Short stories are their own form and I don't personally see them as a stepping stone on the way to a novel but any writing is good practice and skills picked up are cumulative, just like how writing poetry or radio plays or journalism would inform writing a novel too, in different ways.

Do you think writers have a social role to play in society or is their role solely artistic?
I wonder about this and as I get older, the chicken/egg scenario of where art may influence society or society may influence art is not as important as whether the artist is consciously creating.

Tell us something about your latest publication, please.
My most recent novel was *Skin*, released in autumn 2019. A literal and metaphorical voyage to self-acceptance for the protagonist, Natalie, a woman who travels to find a sense of meaning and purpose to her life while overcoming the struggles of binge-eating disorder and low self-esteem.

Can writing be taught?
The technical skills and craft can be improved with reading and practice but the authentic desire to write and to express something, the channelling that happens with this and then the urge to share this with others, offering it out there to the world – that craic has got more of a mystical drive to it. I don't know if that part can be taught.

Have you given or attended creative writing workshops and if you have, share your experiences a bit, please.
I love learning and have attended many writing workshops over the years. I also love facilitating. Currently, I'm developing creative flow workshops with musician Donal McConnon, immersive flow sessions with movement, music, art and stream of consciousness writing. They're

really powerful and dynamic with an emphasis on being present and trusting the process. They're also a lot of fun and the work being generated from them is beautiful.

Finally, what question do you wish that someone would ask about your writing, and how would you answer it?

What would you thank writing for?

For the path it has given me to connect to my essential nature, the incentive to be aware of my life as it happens and the freedom I now have to navigate my days and the world on my terms.

Artist's Statement

Cover image: *not dealing with the important stuff*, by Milda Titford

Milda Titford has drawn, sculpted and painted all her life. After completing a BA (Hons) in Fine arts with a 1st class degree, she extensively painted and exhibited in the UK at the Pump House in Cheltenham and at the Guildhall Arts Centre in Gloucester. She has also exhibited at galleries in London such as the Pump House, the Mafuji, the Arcola and Century.

Biographical Details

Sara Backer's first book of poetry, *Such Luck* (Flowstone Press) follows two poetry chapbooks: *Scavenger Hunt* (dancing girl press) and *Bicycle Lotus* (Left Fork). Her honours include a prize in the 2019 Plough Poetry Prize Competition, nine Pushcart nominations, and fellowships from the Norton Island and Djerassi resident artist programmes. She reads for *The Maine Review*. Recent publications include *Lake Effect, Slant, CutBank, Poetry Northwest*, and *Kenyon Review*.

Ivy Bannister has published a collection of stories, a memoir and a book of poems.

Peter Branson is a poet and singer/songwriter whose poetry has been published widely, including in *Acumen, Agenda, Ambit, Envoi, London Magazine, North, Prole, Warwick Review, Iota,* High Window, *Frogmore Papers, Interpreter's House, Poetry Salzburg Review, Butcher's Dog, SOUTH, Crannóg* and *THE SHOp. Red Hill, Selected Poems* was published in 2013 by Lapwing, Belfast. *Hawk Rising*, also Lapwing, was published in 2016. He was shortlisted for a recent Poetry Business Pamphlet & Collection Competition, and was first prize winner in the 2019/21 Sentinel Poetry Book Competition.

Daragh Byrne has been published in *The Honest Ulsterman, The Blue Nib, Crossways Literary Magazine, The Canberra Times* and *Westerly*, amongst others. In 2021, he won 2nd place in the Allingham Poetry Prize, was awarded Highly Commended in the Winchester Poetry Prize and won 1st prize in the inaugural Rafferty's Return Arts Festival poetry competition. He is the convener of the Sydney Poetry Lounge, a long-running open mic night.

Justine Carbery is a writer, journalist and lecturer in Creative Writing. She is a book critic with *the Sunday Independent* and her short stories have been published in various anthologies and literary journals, including *New Word Order, New Tricks With Matches* and *Herstory*.

Eileen Casey's work is widely published. Fiction prizes include Hennessy/Sunday Tribune, poetry awards include a Patrick and Katherine Kavanagh Fellowship and The Oliver Goldsmith International Poetry Prize, among others. She's published six poetry collections (New Island/Arlen House), a debut short story collection (Arlen House) and a collection of essays (Arlen House). *Treasure*, a short film featuring Casey's bog poetry was commissioned by Offaly Arts for Culture Night 2022 and received a Project Development Award from The Arts Council. Her work is widely published in anthologies by Faber & Faber, Dedalus, and *The Nordic Irish Studies Journal*, among others.

Rachel Coventry's poems are published in *The Rialto, The North, The Moth, THE SHOp, Abridged, Poetry Ireland Review, Cyphers,* and *Crannóg*. Her second collection *The Detachable Heart* was published by Salmon Poetry in 2022.

Bernie Crawford's poetry has been published in Irish and international journals. Her first full collection *Living Water* was published by Chaffinch Press in 2021. She was awarded an arts bursary by Galway County Council in 2019. She is one of the three co-editors of the popular poetry magazine *Skylight 47*.

Timothy Dodd is the author of the poetry collection *Modern Ancient* (The High Window Press), and short story collection *Fissures and Other Stories* (Bottom Dog Press). Forthcoming in 2022 are a second collection of short stories, *Men in Midnight Bloom* (Cowboy Jamboree Press), as well as a joint collection, *Mortality Birds* (with Steve Lambert, Southernmost Books). His poetry has appeared in *Crab Creek Review*, *Roanoke Review*, *Crannóg*, and elsewhere. timothybdodd.wordpress.com.

Barbara Dunne's work has been published in *Circa*, *Skylight 47*, *Vox Galvia*, and *The Avocet: A Journal of Nature Poems*. Her poetry has been published in two anthologies of work by the Oughterard Writers Group, *Shadows* and *Opening Up*. She has been longlisted for the Over The Edge Writer of the Year 2019, and was a finalist in the Cúirt Open Slam 2019. In 2021, she received writing bursaries from Poetry Ireland and the IWC. She is working on her first poetry collection.

Geraint Ellis is a Barbican Young Poet and former Scottish National Slam Poetry finalist. He has been published by *Flipped Eye* and in *The Waxed Lemon*. He has written extensively for BBC Radio 4 Comedy.

Attracta Fahy won the Trócaire Poetry Ireland Poetry Competition in 2021. She was shortlisted for: the Fish International Poetry Competition, the OTE 2018 New Writer, the Allingham Poetry competition in 2019 and 2020, and the Write By The Sea Writing Competition in 2021. Her poems have been published in many magazines and anthologies at home and abroad. Fly on the Wall Poetry published her bestselling debut chapbook collection *Dinner in the Fields* in March 2020. She is presently working towards a full collection.

Jessamyn Fairfield is a Pushcart-nominated writer whose work has previously appeared in *Crannóg*, *Consilience*, and *Kelp Journal*. She recently completed the MA in Writing at the National University of Ireland Galway.

Mary Melvin Geoghegan has five collections of poetry published. Her latest collection *As Moon and Mother Collide* was published by Salmon in 2018. *There Are Only a Few Things* will be published with Salmon in 2023. Her work has been published widely including *Crannóg*, *Poetry Ireland Review*, *The Stinging Fly*, *The Moth*, *Skylight47*, *Orbis184*, *Cyphers*, *The Stony Thursday Book*, Hodges Figgis Anthology, *Poems on the Dart*, *Live Encounters*. She was shortlisted for the Fish Poetry Award, the Franicis Ledwidge prize, the Cúirt New Writing award, the Jonathan Swift Poetry Award in 2019 and 2020 and for the Desmond O'Grady International Poetry Award and Poem for Patience in 2022.

Mark Granier's work has been broadcast on RTÉ and appeared in numerous outlets, including *Crannóg*, *Poetry Review*, *The New Statesman*, *The TLS* and Carol

Ann Duffy's online pandemic project/archive, *Write Where We Are Now*. His fifth book, *Ghostlight: New & Selected Poems*, was published by Salmon Poetry in 2017.

Brian Harrington holds a BA in Irish and English from NUI Galway and an MLitt in Psychology from University College Dublin. He has co-authored psychological research in journals such as *Computers in Human Behaviour*.

Rachael Hegarty's debut, *Flight Paths Over Finglas* (Salmon, 2017) won the Shine Strong Award in 2018. Her *May Day 1974* (Salmon, 2019) and *Dancing with Memory* (Salmon, 2021) earned national and international acclaim. Her next collection, *Wild Flowers Made Me* will be launched in 2023.

Kevin Higgins is co-organiser of Over The Edge literary events in Galway. He has published six full collections of poems. His poems also feature in *Identity Parade – New British and Irish Poets* (Bloodaxe, 2010) and in *The Hundred Years' War: Modern War Poems* (Bloodaxe 2014). *The Selected Satires of Kevin Higgins* was published by NuaScéalta in 2016. *The Minister For Poetry Has Decreed* was published by Culture Matters (UK) also in 2016. His work has been broadcast on RTÉ Radio, Lyric FM, and BBC Radio 4. His extended essay *Thrills & Difficulties: Being A Marxist Poet In 21st Century Ireland* was published in pamphlet form by Beir Bua Press in 2021.

Mary Ellen Hodgins' work has been published in several publications including: *Cyphers, THE SHOp, The Clare Champion, Revival, The Galway Review, Live Encounters*. She has published one collection of poems.

Michael Lyle is the author of the poetry chapbook *The Everywhere of Light* (Plan B Press, 2018) and his poems have appeared widely, including in *Atlanta Review, The Carolina Quarterly, The Hollins Critic, Mudfish, The Madrigal* and *Poetry East*. He was longlisted for the Fish Poetry Prize in 2020 and 2021.

Antoinette McCarthy has been shortlisted for the Francis MacManus short story competition, the Over the Edge short story competition and the Lilliput Press culture night short story competition.

Peggy McCarthy won the Fish Poetry Prize in 2020. She was shortlisted for the Gregory O'Donoghue Poetry Competition in 2022, the Trim Poetry Competition in 2022, and the Wells Poetry Competition in 2020. She won third place in the Goldsmith Poetry Prize in 2021 and was Highly Commended in the Desmond O'Grady Poetry Competition in 2022 and the Francis Ledwidge Competition in 2021. Her poems have been published in *Hold Open the Door* from the Ireland Chair of Poetry, *Southword*, and *Cork Words*. She was one of ten poets selected to participate in a workshop with Paul Muldoon at the Kinsale Arts Weekend in July 2022. She holds an MA in Creative Writing from UCC.

Karen J McDonnell's *Driftwood* was shortlisted for Poem of the Year at the 2021 Irish Book Awards. Her work is widely published and Pushcart & Best of the Net nominated. She is working on her next poetry collection for which she received an

Arts Council of Ireland Agility Award. Her debut collection, *This Little World*, is published by Doire Press. karenjmcdonnell.com

Laura McKee's first poetry pamphlet is due in spring 2023 with Against the Grain Press. She is currently studying for an MA with The Poetry School and Newcastle University. This year she has been commended in the Hippocrates Prize, and longlisted in The Rialto Nature and Place Competition. @LauraMcKee_fyeh

Alan McMonagle has written for radio and published two collections of short stories, *Psychotic Episodes*, published by Arlen House and *Liar Liar,* published by Wordsonthestreet. *Ithaca*, his first novel, was published by Picador in 2017 and was longlisted for the Desmond Elliott Award for first novels, the Dublin Literary Award, and shortlisted for an Irish Book Award. His second novel, *Laura Cassidy's Walk Of Fame,* appeared in 2020.

Lourdes Mackey has been published in *The Irish Times, the Irish Examiner, Cork Words 2* and in the online journal *Flashback Fiction*. Her story on Charlotte Despard is included in the UEA's Suffragette Stories. Her short fiction has been listed in the Penguin Ireland Short Story Competition, the From the Well Short Story Award and the Colm Tóibín International Short Story Competition. She is a regular contributor to RTÉ radio's *Sunday Miscellany*.

DS Maolalai has received nine nominations for Best of the Net and seven for the Pushcart Prize. His poetry has been released in three collections, *Love is Breaking Plates in the Garden* (Encircle Press, 2016), *Sad Havoc Among the Birds* (Turas Press, 2019) and *Noble Rot* (Turas Press, 2022).

Marie Marchand is Poet Laureate of Ellensburg, Washington. Her poetry has been published in *Catamaran Literary Reader, California Quarterly, Paterson Literary Review, Tiny Seed Journal*, and *High Plains Register*. Her new book *Gifts to the Attentive* was published in May 2022 by Winter Goose Publishing. mishiepoet.com and @mishiepoet.

Katherine Meehan's work has appeared in *The Moth, The Kenyon Review, One Hand Clapping, Bath Magg, Ink, Sweat & Tears*, and other journals.

Geraldine Mitchell has published four collections of poetry, her most recent being *Mute/Unmute*, published by Arlen House in 2020. She was placed second in the Troubadour International Poetry Prize in 2021 and is a former winner of the Patrick Kavanagh Award.

Anne O'Brien's stories have been shortlisted for the Bridport Prize, the RA & Pin Drop Short Story Award, BBC Opening Lines, the London Magazine and FISH. She was awarded the 2021 Wasafiri Life Writing Prize and is also a past winner of the Bath Short Story Award.

Jean O'Brien's sixth collection *Stars Burn Regardless* was published by Salmon Poetry in 2022, she was the November Poet in Residence in the Centre Culturel

Irlandais in Paris in 2021 and was commissioned to write a poem for Co. Laois's Poetry in a Van festival. Her commissioned poem *Sustenance* was recently published in the Brazilian Journal of Irish Studies dedicated to Eavan Boland.

Jamie O'Halloran won 2nd place in the 2021 Fool for Poetry Chapbook Competition. Her poems have appeared recently in *Southword*, *One Hand Clapping*, *The Honest Ulsterman*, *Skylight 47*, and the anthology *Local Wonders*. One of her poems is included in the 2022 Creative Ireland Poetry Anthology. Her poetry reviews can be found in *The Laurel Review*, *LitPub*, and *The Tupelo Quarterly*.

Ciaran O'Rourke's first collection, *The Buried Breath*, was highly commended by the Forward Foundation in 2019. His second collection, *Phantom Gang*, is forthcoming from The Irish Pages Press, and *American Epic: On Paterson* is available as a pamphlet from Beir Bua Press.

Triin Paja has published three poetry collections in Estonian and has won the Juhan Liiv Poetry Prize, the Betti Alver Literary Award, and the Värske Rõhk Poetry Award. Her English poetry has received a Pushcart Prize and can be found in *The Prairie Schooner*, *Cincinnati Review*, *Rattle*, *Pleiades*, *Room*, and elsewhere.

Susan Rich is an award-winning poet and essayist. She is the author of *Gallery of Postcards and Maps: New and Selected Poems*, *Cloud Pharmacy*, *The Alchemist's Kitchen*, *Cures Include Travel* and *The Cartographer's Tongue /Poems of the World*. Her poems appear in *Alaska Quarterly Review*, *Crannóg*, and *Poetry Ireland Review* among other journals. Her new collection, *Blue Atlas*, is forthcoming from Red Hen Press in 2024. http://www.poetsusanrich.com

Anne Ryland's third collection of poetry, *Unruled Journal*, was recently published by Valley Press. Her previous books are *Autumnologist*, shortlisted for The Forward Prize for Best First Collection 2006, and *The Unmothering Class*, a New Writing North Read Regional choice. She leads community-based writing workshops in Northumberland and the Scottish Borders. https://anneryland.co.uk

Shannon Savvas won the Fish Short Story Prize (2021/22), the Cúirt New Writing Prize (2019), Flash500 FF (2019), and Reflex Fiction (2017). She was shortlisted for the Cúirt New Writing Prize (2022) and longlisted in 2021 for the Bridport Prize. www.shannonsavvas.com/

Cassie Smith-Christmas holds a PhD from the University of Glasgow and her writing has appeared in *The New Word Order*; *Tangled Locks*; *The Milk House*; *The Wild Word*; *Gutter*; *Poets' Republic*, and *Earthlines*. Her novel *Silent Cicadas* was a runner-up in the Irish Writers Centre's Novel Fair 2022.

David Starkey served as Santa Barbara's 2009-2011 poet laureate. He is founding director of the Creative Writing Program at Santa Barbara City College, co-editor of *The California Review of Books,* and the Publisher and co-editor of Gunpowder Press. Over the past thirty-five years, he has published ten full-length collections of poetry with small presses — most recently *Dance, You Monster, to My Soft Song*, winner of the 2021 FutureCycle Press Poetry Book Award, and *What Just Happened: 210 Haiku Against the Trump Presidency*.

Noelle Sullivan's poems have appeared in *Abridged, Bealtaine, Crannóg*, and other Irish journals. *NEW GRASS ON THE GOLDEN SUNLIGHT MINE*, her first chapbook, was published in 2022 by Open Country Press.

Martin Towers has been recently published in *The Galway Review* and *Amethyst Review*.

Niamh Twomey's work has appeared in journals and anthologies such as *Local Wonders: Poems of Our Immediate Surrounds, Southword*, and *New Irish Writing*, among others. She won the 2022 Trim Poetry Competition.

Brigitte de Valk won the Cúirt New Writing Prize in 2020, and the Royal Holloway Art Writing Competition. She was awarded second place in the Benedict Kiely Short Story Competition and was longlisted for the Alpine Fellowship Writing Prize 2020. Her entry to the Bournemouth Writing Prize in 2021 and 2022 was selected for publication. Brigitte's short fiction is also published by *Sans. PRESS, Happy London Press* and *Reflex Press*.

Steve Wade's short story collection, *In Fields of Butterfly Flames and Other Stories*, was published in October 2020 by Bridge House Publishing. His fiction has been published and anthologised in over fifty print publications. His short stories have been placed and shortlisted in numerous writing competitions, including the Francis MacManus Awards and Hennessy New Irish Writing. Winner of the Short Story category in the Write By the Sea Writing Competition in 2019, and four times First Prize winner in the Delvin Garradrimna Book Fair Competition. He won first prize in the Dún Laoghaire/Rathdown Writing Competition in 2020. www.stephenwade.ie

Dolores Walshe has been a prizewinner in the Cáirde Short Story Award 2021, Sean O'Faoláin Short Story Award and Francis MacManus Awards 2015/09. She was awarded the Berlin Writing Prize 2017/18 and has twice received an Arts Council Bursary. She's also won the Bryan MacMahon Short Story Award at Listowel Writers' Week. Her award-winning plays have been published by Syracuse University Press NY, 2014 and Carysfort Press Dublin, 2008. She has also had a novel and short story collection published by Wolfhound Press. Her poetry has been published by *Crannóg* and Hungry Hill's *Poets Meet Politics*.

Stay in touch with
Crannóg
@
www.crannogmagazine.com

Lightning Source UK Ltd.
Milton Keynes UK
UKHW051215150922
408911UK00007B/208